So You Want To Be A Private Investigator

A Step-by-Step Guide on How to Begin

By

Chris Jennings and Mike Jennings

MAPLE
PUBLISHERS

So You Want To Be A Private Investigator

Author: Chris Jennings and Mike Jennings

Copyright © 2025 Chris Jennings and Mike Jennings

The author asserts the moral right to be identified as the author of this work.

The right of Chris Jennings and Mike Jennings to be identified as author of this work has been asserted by the author in accordance with section 77 and 78 of the Copyright, Designs and Patents Act 1988.

First Published in 2025

ISBN 978-1-83538-701-6 (Paperback)
      978-1-83538-702-3 (E-Book)

Book Layout by:
    White Magic Studios
    www.whitemagicstudios.co.uk

Published by:
    Maple Publishers
    Fairbourne Drive, Atterbury,
    Milton Keynes,
    MK10 9RG, UK
    www.maplepublishers.com

A CIP catalogue record for this title is available from the British Library.

All rights reserved. No part of this book may be reproduced or translated in any form or by any means, electronic or mechanical, including photocopying, recording or by any information storage and retrieval system without written permission from the author.

Foreword

My dear aspirant of the clandestine arts,

Should you find yourself leafing through these pages with the fervent ambition of one day donning the mantle of Private Investigator, then be advised: you stand at the threshold of an occupation at once exhilarating and exacting.

Let this book serve not merely as a manual of methods, but as a cautionary companion—reminding you that every skill demands responsibility, that every revelation must be tempered by respect for the lives touched by your enquiries.

If you embrace these teachings with diligence and humility, you may yet earn the satisfaction of unravelling mysteries that perplex the keenest minds. You will stand, in moments of triumph, upon the precipice of the unknown—and there, with nerves steeled and intellect keen, you will peer into the heart of enigma and command it to reveal its secrets.

Proceed, then, with keen eye, steady hand and the wisdom contained within this excellent tome always to hand. May your deductions be sound, your courage resolute, and your conscience ever your guiding star.

I remain, in admiration of your enterprise,

Sherlock Holmes

P.S. Having chronicled Holmes's finest cases, I can assure you this book - So you want to be a Private Investigator - will prove an indispensable companion on your own investigative adventures.

— Dr John H. Watson

Contents

Foreword 3

Introduction 5

Chapter One – Starting Your Business 7

Chapter Two – Client Management 23

Chapter Three – Invoicing 32

Chapter Four – Process Serving 39

Chapter Five – Report Writing 50

Chapter Six – Interviewing Witnesses 56

Chapter Seven – Witness Statements 65

Chapter Eight – Open Source Intelligence 76

Chapter Nine – Cyber Security 87

Chapter Ten – Surveillance Law and Procedure 97

Chapter Eleven – Electronic Surveillance 112

Chapter Twelve – Static Surveillance 121

Chapter Thirteen – Foot Surveillance 131

Chapter Fourteen – Mobile Surveillance 144

Chapter Fifteen – And Finally 157

Introduction

Stepping into the Shadows

Have you ever watched a detective unravel a mystery on screen and thought, "I could do that?". Or perhaps you've found yourself piecing together clues in your own life, whether it's figuring out who nicked the last biscuit or why your mate's been acting suspiciously lately, and realised you've got a knack for it. If so, the world of private investigation might just be calling your name. Welcome to 'So You Want to Be a Private Investigator', your guide to turning that curiosity into a career right here in the UK.

Being a private investigator isn't all trench coats and smoky offices though, admittedly, a good coat never hurts. It's a job that blends sharp observation, relentless determination and a touch of creativity, all while navigating the unique rules and realities of the UK landscape. From tracking down missing persons to digging into corporate fraud, this is a profession where no two days are the same. But here's the kicker, it's not for everyone. It takes grit, patience and a willingness to ask the questions others shy away from.

We wrote this book because we've been where you are – standing at the edge, wondering what it takes to step into this secretive, often misunderstood trade. Over the years, we've chased leads through rainy streets, sifted through mountains of paperwork, and learned the hard way what works and what doesn't work (and what lands you in hot water). Now we are here to share that with you. Whether you're a complete beginner or someone with a little bit of experience looking to go pro, this book is your roadmap to getting started in the UK. It's a beginning.

Whilst trying to keep things simple, there are some aspects to this line of work where a degree of detail is necessary. There are other very good books out there that will go into much more detail around the more specialised areas such as surveillance and open source intelligence gathering but in this book we have endeavoured to provide the basics across a broad section of everything you need to get started. In the spirit of keeping things simple and straightforward we have followed a standard format of identifying learning outcomes at the start of each chapter and included a knowledge refresher check at the end, along with some recommended reading suggestions where you can learn more about the subject covered in that chapter in more detail.

We'll cover the lot: what the job really entails, the skills you'll need, the legal ins and outs (because trust us, you don't want to fall foul of the law), and, crucially, how to build a business that stands out from the rest. You'll hear about the tools of the trade – some high-tech, some as simple as a notepad – and get practical tips on everything from surveillance to client meetings. Along the way, we will throw in a few stories from the field because if there's one thing this job teaches you, it's that truth is often stranger than fiction.

So, if you're ready to swap the armchair for the driver's seat, to trade guesswork for evidence, and to step into a career where every case is a puzzle waiting to be solved, then turn the page. The world of private investigation is waiting and it's got a spot for you.

Chapter One
Starting Your Business

Introduction

Starting your own business can be a daunting prospect at the best of times, particularly if it is in a new field of professional practice where you have no previous experience to fall back on and few, if any, professional contacts. There can be many pitfalls along the way.

It may be that you have spotted a gap in the market, either because there is nobody else doing it or because there is room for further development and original thinking. Or it may be that you are approaching retirement in one profession where the skills acquired over a long career could prove lucrative once transferred to a new but related area. Equally, it may be that you would like to make your 'side hustle' your day job. It would be fair to say that many people working as private investigators often come from a related background, such as the military or the police. Whatever the reasons and whatever your background, it is vitally important to understand the industry you'll be working in. Before you jump straight in, take the time to step back and do some market research. Which sector are you going into? Who will your competitors be? Who is your ideal customer? What value can you add that your competitors don't?

In this chapter we will look at some of the first steps to consider before setting up your own business, be that as a private investigator or anything else – the lessons are all the same.

Learning Outcomes

By the end of this chapter you will have a good understanding of some of the key steps to consider when setting up your own business including:

- Conducting proper market research.
- Deciding on the most appropriate business structures for your circumstances.
- The importance of getting your business branding right.
- Having an effective business plan.
- Getting your finances in order.
- Choosing the most appropriate location.
- Pulling together an effective marketing strategy.

Step 1: Research! Research! Research!

In setting up any new venture, it's crucial to comprehend not only what you're selling but also to whom you're selling. This encompasses not only your core business and audience but also your unique selling points (or USPs). What sets you apart from your competitors? Understanding your target audience's interests, motivations and behaviours will be invaluable when it comes to branding and marketing your business.

At this early stage, it's beneficial to approach the task from the perspective of your future clients. Imagine how someone would discover your business, become a paying client and potentially become a repeat client. Put yourself in their shoes and consider how they might interact with your business.

A Strengths, Weaknesses, Opportunities, Threats (SWOT) analysis may seem daunting, but it's an effective way to document these traits. Essentially, it involves creating four lists under each heading. This approach allows you to develop a plan to capitalise on your opportunities and prepare for potential challenges.

Step 2: Be Clear on Your Structure

At the outset of establishing your business, you have many options, but choose carefully – the structure you choose will significantly impact your liability for tax, which in turn impacts upon the risk to your personal assets and your access to business finance. Registration isn't mandatory to make your business official, but you must at least notify HMRC.

Here are the six most common business structures:

1. **Sole Trader (Self-Employed).** If you're an individual and run your own business, you can register as a sole trader. This means you retain all your business profits after paying tax on them. However, you're personally liable for any losses incurred by the business. HMRC provides a calculator to help you budget for your tax payments as a sole trader.

2. **Limited Company.** A limited company can be classified as either limited by shares or limited by guarantee. A limited by shares company typically operates for profit, has shareholders and can retain any profits after paying tax. In contrast, a limited by guarantee company has guarantors instead of shareholders and reinvests profits back into the company. These organisations are commonly known as 'not for profit'. Limited companies will commonly operate under a trading name, which is usually the same as the business's

name. This structure offers numerous long-term options in terms of finance as well as access to specialised financing schemes specifically for small businesses and start-ups, such as R&D tax credits for those businesses where innovation is a feature.

3. **A Business Partnership.** When two or more entrepreneurs collaborate, they form a business partnership. In this arrangement, individuals share responsibility for the business's operations, including losses, costs and profits.

4. **A Limited Liability Partnership (LLP).** An LLP is merely a legal entity with a separate identity from its constituent members. Changes in the LLP's membership do not affect its continued existence. LLPs combine the flexibility of a business partnership with the added benefits of limited liability for its members. As an LLP, the business will be the owner of its assets and, therefore, is liable for its debts, while members act as agents and are only liable up to their contributions.

5. **A Social Enterprise.** A social enterprise is a business established to serve people or communities. It can operate as a limited company, charity, cooperative, sole trader, business partnership or community interest company (CIC). Each category has specific rules governing business operations, so it's important when setting up a business to carefully consider which one aligns most closely with your business goals.

6. **An Unincorporated Association.** An unincorporated association is a group of individuals who come together for non-profit purposes. Most typically this will include voluntary organisations or sports clubs. While not a business entity, members are responsible for any debts or obligations incurred by the association. If the association then decides to engage in trading activities and generate profits, it must pay taxes and submit tax returns in the usual way.

Step 3: Your Business Branding

Your name and brand identity significantly reflect your business's essence, especially when you're just starting out. First impressions are fleeting but can shape a customer's long-term relationship with your business. Being instantly recognisable helps to build your brand identity and instil trust. Leverage the research you conducted on your industry, competitors and market to select a name, logo and branding that aligns with your vision. Consider the following tips for choosing a name:

- Keep it simple and memorable.
- Ensure it's easy to pronounce and spell.
- Avoid confusion with similar names.
- Conduct a thorough online search to check availability.
- Verify if someone else is already using your name or if it's available for a website domain or social media handles.
- Perform a quick search to ensure your name is accessible across various platforms.
- Copying someone else's name or using something too similar could lead to copyright infringement, passing off or trademark infringement.

Design your logo, which serves as your business's symbol and sets it apart from the competition. It defines your brand and influences everything you do, from the first thing employees, connections and potential clients see to the overall 'look and feel' of your business. Consider your messaging and how your logo relates to your offerings. Think about the desired positioning of your business and how your logo aligns with it. Some other factors to consider will include:

- Choose brand colours that complement the overall 'look and feel' of your business. Opt for a limited palette to maximise impact (and minimise cost).
- Ensure your logo is unique to avoid legal issues such as copyright infringement, passing off or trademark infringement.
- Create different variations of your logo for various platforms, including social media, the web and other marketing materials.
- Take advantage of free and affordable tools available to help you design and implement your brand identity.

Don't fret if you're not a graphic design expert! There are numerous free and user-friendly tools available online to assist you in getting started, or you could seek help from creative friends or family.

Create Your Brand Guidelines

Brand guidelines regulate and standardise your 'shop window', that is, how your business should be represented to the wider world, encompassing your visual identity, communication style and more. They include your mission statement, values, logo usage, colour palette, tone of voice and other relevant details. There are many creative examples of brand guidelines online, but a concise document can serve as an excellent reference point, especially when you're managing your business. It's an excellent way to gain clarity on your branding from the very beginning. This activity allows you to view your brand as a whole and refine how you want to portray your business.

Your 'brand story' must be succinct. No more than a few sentences. What is your purpose or mission statement? What are your goals? What are your values? What is your tagline or strap-line? What is your brand positioning? This is sometimes referred to as the 'elevator pitch', hence the importance of being succinct!

Your Visual Style

Identify your primary and secondary brand colours. Don't forget to include red, green and blue (RGB) colours for web use and cyan, magenta, yellow and black (CMYB) colours for print. Specify the fonts you'll use and how they'll be applied. Determine the imagery your business will use. How will your branding be reflected in your online presence, such as your website and any digital advertising?

Your Logo

Are there any variations of your logo? Outline how your logo should be used. Specify any rules for sizing and spacing. As your business grows, it's essential to regularly review and update your branding to ensure it remains aligned with your current business journey.

Your Tone of Voice

Describe the sound of your brand. Identify the words or phrases that resonate with your business. Do you have any overarching messages? Provide a description of your tone of voice.

Protect Your Branding

Once you have done the hard work of creating an eye-catching logo and catchy product name, what prevents someone from stealing them? Trademarking can serve as a protective measure for your intellectual property. It encompasses logos, colours, and words. The government's website provides comprehensive information on the process of registering a trademark in the UK and the criteria for eligibility. Additionally, you can conduct a search to determine if an item has already been trademarked.

Step 4: Write Your Business Plan

A business plan is a written document that provides a concise overview of your business. It outlines your objectives, strategies, sales and marketing projections, and financial forecasts. This document serves as a valuable summary of your business, effectively communicating your ideas and aspirations to potential customers, suppliers or even staff.

Understanding the importance of a business plan offers several benefits. It helps you visualise your long-term and short-term goals and objectives, enabling you to measure your progress and performance. It clarifies your business concept or proposal, helping you identify potential challenges before they arise. Moreover, it provides insights into how your business can grow and thrive.

A well-crafted business plan should encompass seven key sections:

1. **Executive summary.** This section provides a brief overview of your business, highlighting its unique value proposition and potential for growth.
2. **Business description.** This section delves into the details of your business, including its structure, operations, and market position.
3. **Market strategies.** This section outlines your approach to market research, segmentation, and targeting, ensuring that your business effectively positions itself in the market.
4. **Competitor analysis.** This section examines your competitors, analysing their strengths, weaknesses, and market positioning to identify opportunities for differentiation and growth.
5. **Product and service design and development plan.** This section outlines the process of designing and developing your products or services, ensuring that they meet customer needs and market demands.
6. **Operations and management plan.** This section provides details about your business operations, including your management structure, staffing requirements and processes for efficient execution.
7. **Financial information, planning and factors.** This section presents financial projections, including revenue, expenses and profitability, as well as key financial planning considerations and factors that may impact your business's success.

If you're considering applying for a start-up loan, it's essential to have a well-prepared business plan. Banks and finance providers often require business plans as part of their loan assessment process, as they provide valuable insights into the viability and potential success of your business. To get started on your business plan, consider the following:

- **Summary.** Provide a concise overview of your business, highlighting its unique value proposition and potential for growth.
- **Background.** Explain your motivation for starting a business, your qualifications, education and work experience, and any relevant training courses that could enhance your business skills.
- **Products and services.** Describe the products or services you'll be selling, including their features, benefits and target market.
- **Finances.** Outline the costs associated with each product or service, including supplier and manufacturer payments, staff expenses, premises costs, bills and other outgoings. Provide financial projections for the next twelve months.

Remember, a well-crafted business plan is a crucial tool for planning, executing and achieving your business goals.

Step 5: Figure Out Your Finances

Being the owner of your own business can be a wonderful thing but it also comes with responsibility and it means you'll be responsible for its finances. It can be a daunting prospect, but balancing your books and keeping control of the numbers is crucial to success. Without that you are on a slippery slope!

One way to manage your finances effectively is to open a separate business bank account. While it's common to use a personal account for business purposes when self-employed, there are several benefits to having a dedicated business bank account. It's important to note that some banks prohibit using personal accounts for business purposes, so it's crucial to check your bank's terms of service before opening a business bank account.

Firstly, it saves time and improves money management by separating personal and business finances from the start. This separation makes it easier to identify business-related transactions and ensures that your accounting tasks are streamlined.

Secondly, having a business bank account makes tax deadlines much more manageable. By keeping your business finances separate, you can easily track and manage your expenses, making it easier to prepare for tax obligations.

Another option to consider is hiring an accountant. Accountants can provide valuable assistance with bookkeeping, tax advice and compliance, reducing the stress of managing your business's finances. However, hiring an accountant can be costly, especially for startups. As a startup, it may be more practical to manage your own finances and track expenses using spreadsheets or online accounting software.

The Importance of Terms and Conditions

Terms and Conditions (more commonly referred to as T&Cs) are an essential agreement which form the legal basis upon which businesses engage with each other and their customers. Whilst it is not a legal requirement for your business to have a set of written T&Cs, in the event of a dispute with a customer, client or supplier, your business will be in a much stronger position if armed with a robust set of terms to rely on. If a new business is set up without a set of standard terms, it will be difficult to clearly show what they have agreed to provide or illustrate that a customer, client or supplier has breached your terms.

What Should be Included?

A typical set of T&Cs may include:

- The relevant law governing the transaction.
- Payment terms, including when payment will fall due.
- Consequences of late payment, such as details of any interest which will accrue.
- Any relevant guarantees or warranties.
- A clear explanation of what products or services you are providing.
- Any timelines for delivery of the product or services.
- What action can be taken if you do not deliver the goods or the customer does not pay promptly.

There is no 'one size fits all' approach to what terms and conditions a business should have and these should be tailored to the specifics of your business, but having a clear and robust set of T&Cs will avoid ambiguity and misunderstanding about what services you are providing, and the reciprocal obligations owed by your business, your clients, customers and suppliers.

Are Terms and Conditions Legally Binding?

The short answer is no. Terms and Conditions (T&Cs) are not automatically legally binding. When compared with contracts themselves, T&Cs are often not signed and accepted in the same way, so their enforceability is often misunderstood. For them to be legally binding, they must have already been accepted by the customer or client in the transaction, so it is recommended that your T&Cs are signed by your clients, customers or suppliers before you begin your engagement. If it is the case the customer did not need to accept the T&Cs before entering the transaction, then they may not be bound by them. Without them, businesses will have to provide sufficient evidence to demonstrate that their terms of business have been legally incorporated in their contracts and dealings with clients, customers or suppliers. This can be difficult and expensive to prove.

Where a business does not have a written set of contractual terms, this may also appear less professional to prospective customers or clients.

The Importance of T&Cs: The Three C's

Certainty

Written T&Cs provide certainty and are much easier to enforce. It is also much easier to establish when there has been a breach of the terms. If you have a clear and robust set of T&Cs this will lessen the scope for ambiguity and, naturally, lessens the likelihood of disputes arising. Preparing a standard set of terms from the outset will be much cheaper than being involved in a lengthy and costly litigation process.

Clarity

T&Cs give clarity about what should happen in any given scenario. They clearly set out the key terms which govern the parties to the contract and help both parties understand their duties, rights, roles and responsibilities.

Confidence (and Consistency)

Having a clear set of T&Cs means businesses can maintain a consistent approach whilst also delivering a good customer service. Having an agreed set of terms avoids ambiguity and helps manage client expectations about the goods and services businesses have agreed to provide. It will also give clients confidence in knowing what happens with regards to delivery and payment, so they know what rights they have in the event of late delivery, for example.

Invoicing Customers

We will look at invoicing in more detail in Chapter Three, but it is an important aspect of starting a business and to get right from the outset so it is worth devoting some time to it here also. An invoice details the costs and payment expectations for a job. To avoid confusion, it's best to lay out your terms and conditions upfront or before signing a contract with a client. Well-defined invoices don't just keep you legally covered, they're also vital for tracking your finances. They play a key role in managing books, filing taxes and handling accounting tasks. For clients who don't pay immediately, setting up a consistent invoicing process and sticking to it is a must. Whether you're tackling a single freelance project or ongoing contract work, mastering the art of crafting a clear, professional invoice quickly helps guarantee you get paid for your efforts.

One frequent hazard for new businesses is excessive flexibility in invoicing. Inconsistent payments can lead to cash flow problems, leaving you uncertain and unprepared for unexpected expenses or hindering growth planning. To avoid these pitfalls, it's essential to:

- Clearly define what you'll charge customers for.
- Set limits on the services you provide.
- Be transparent about your expected payment terms and due dates.

When considering financing your business idea, a start-up loan from the UK government can be a valuable option. Here are some key factors to keep in mind during your application process:

- Understand your business and objectives.
- Present your business effectively and clearly outline your goals for the first year and beyond.
- Be realistic about the amount you want to borrow.
- Ensure that your expenses align with your objectives and avoid overspending.
- Highlight your relevant skills and experience, including any previous business or sector-specific experience.
- Consider the training and formal qualifications required in your industry, but emphasise the value of real-life experience.
- Identify any knowledge gaps and plan for training or mentoring to fill them.

Additionally, it's crucial to have a back-up plan in case of unexpected events. Consider how you would meet your personal expenses, loan repayments and any long-term business liabilities if your business were to fail. Create a personal survival budget, anticipate the worst and set realistic expectations, especially if you're going into business with others.

Step 6: Find Your Place, Find Your Space

You've completed your homework and jumped through all of the legal hoops, and now you're set to check out the perfect spot for your new venture. Whether you're eyeing an office rental, dreaming of a storefront or starting small from your attic room, there are a few key points to consider.

Top of the list, make sure you've got solid insurance in place. No matter where you set up shop, securing the right coverage is a must to protect your business from the unexpected. As you gear up to launch, having a firm grasp on the essentials about your company is vital. This understanding will guide you in picking the right policies, figuring out what insurance you're eligible for and choosing the coverage that fits your business best.

When applying for insurance, providers will typically ask you a series of questions to provide you with a quote and assist you in finding a suitable insurance package. These questions may include:

- Do you want to insure equipment, stock or both?
- Do you want to protect your premises in the event of damage, fire, flood or theft?
- Do you own or rent the building where your business operates?
- Do customers, suppliers or colleagues visit your premises regularly?
- Do you offer a professional service to paying clients?
- Do you want other subsidiaries or associated businesses to be included in the insurance coverage?

Additionally, if you're working from home, consider the number of employees you anticipate having in the next twelve months. It's also a good idea to check with your home insurance provider to ensure that you're adequately covered for any business-related activities that may occur within your home premises.

Property insurance typically covers claims related to your business premises, but there are other types of insurance that may be necessary depending on your business activities. These include:

- **Public liability insurance.** This insurance covers claims involving individuals outside your company.
- **Employers' liability insurance.** If you plan to hire employees, this insurance is a legal requirement.

- **Product liability insurance.** This insurance covers claims related to your products.
- **Professional indemnity insurance.** This insurance covers claims involving your services.

Obtaining the necessary planning permissions is crucial to ensure your business operations align with local rules and regulations, even if you're running things from home. Every property comes with a specific planning designation and you'll need to confirm that your planned activities fall within the permitted use category for your premises. If your neighbours aren't pleased and decide to complain to the local council, you might face enforcement measures that could stop your operations.

If you're working from home, the scale of your business activities could mean you'll need to pay business rates on any section of your property that's mainly or entirely used for work. You can divide the costs, paying council tax for the residential portion and business rates for the business area, though this depends on available exemptions or reliefs. Properties used solely for business purposes will be subject to business rates.

Health and Safety

Health and safety is important no matter where you run your business. Employers are legally obligated to perform a risk assessment, and if you're self-employed and your work could affect others, you need to do one too. For instance, a self-employed person working from home in a space no-one else can access might not be required by law to do a risk assessment, but it's still smart to make sure your setup is safe and doesn't put you in harm's way.

You can do a risk assessment by jotting down potential hazards in your workspace and tweaking things to reduce those risks. Ask yourself the following questions:

- Is there enough space to work comfortably?
- Do I have room for my equipment or storage?
- Can I get in and out of all areas easily?
- Is the lighting good enough?
- Are there things on the floor that could trip me up?
- Is it easy to sit and work for a while without strain?
- Can I reach everything I need without a hassle?

Step 7: Business Promotion

The world of marketing and social media can seem daunting, especially to new business owners, but there are several simple steps you can take when first setting out which can help you embark on your journey:

- Create a comprehensive marketing plan. Initially, creating a marketing plan may seem like a time-consuming task, but it's akin to your business plan. It provides clarity on your objectives and strategies. Without a plan, you'll lack the necessary insights to assess the effectiveness of your marketing efforts and potentially miss out on valuable opportunities for business growth.
- Stay organised and on-track even when life gets hectic. By having a well-defined plan, you'll be well-prepared to handle any challenges that arise and can schedule your activities accordingly.
- Strategically grow your business. A well-executed marketing plan can help you generate new leads, secure sales and anticipate increased demand.
- Proactively seize opportunities rather than reacting to them. By adopting a proactive approach, you'll stay ahead of the curve and capitalise on emerging trends.
- Maximise your budget effectively. As a small business owner, every penny counts. A marketing plan can guide you in allocating your resources wisely and ensuring the best return on your investment.
- Learn from your mistakes. While not everything goes as planned, having a plan in place allows you to quickly identify areas for improvement and make necessary adjustments.
- Ensure compliance with data protection obligations. The Information Commissioner's Office (ICO), the UK's independent body responsible for upholding information rights, has published two comprehensive guides outlining how to comply with the requirements under the Privacy and Electronic Communications Regulations 2003 (as amended) (PECR) for conducting direct marketing via email and live calls. Adhering to these regulations is crucial to avoid potential fines and legal consequences. We will see throughout this book how complying with the law is vital, particularly so in the private investigation business. Getting it right from the outset makes it easier to maintain compliance as you go along. Start how you mean to continue.
- Launch your website. Consider your website as your virtual shopfront. It serves as a platform for potential customers to stay informed about new products and offers, gain insights into your

business and read testimonials. Online website builders make it easy to set up and customise your online storefront. However, it's crucial to conduct thorough research on pricing and features to find the best fit for your business.

- No e-commerce business is complete without secure payment options for customers. Ensure that your website provides safe payment methods for online transactions.

Enhance Your Social Media Presence

Growing a social media following is a cost-effective way to promote your business. A smart, well-planned strategy can help you expand your audience, attract new customers and guide them to your online store.

Use the market research and customer persona we looked at earlier in this chapter to figure out which social media platforms best fit your business. Think about where your target audience hangs out and engages most – maybe they're more active on Facebook, or perhaps X, Snapchat or Instagram is where they thrive.

Before jumping into a social media marketing campaign, take a moment to define your business goals. Are you aiming to boost your reach, drive more traffic to your site or ramp up product sales?

Get Noticed Online

Search engine optimisation (SEO) involves tweaking or enhancing a website's content to boost its visibility on search engines. This encompasses activities like researching keywords, building links, and refining content.

For e-commerce, it's all about regularly applying these techniques to attract more visitors to your online shop. Whether that's the storefront on your website or your product listings on digital marketplaces, staying consistent is crucial. By creating a strategy and making small, steady improvements to your site each week, you'll keep it fresh and effective over time.

Case Study

When I started Cotswold Private Investigations, I was really lucky. I already had experience running a detective agency from scratch, so I thought I knew what it took to run a small business start-up in this field. I also knew the kind of clients and cases I usually worked with, and the services they needed the most. This meant that I knew exactly what kind of client I wanted to work with. I designed my website and services to appeal to them and make them feel comfortable. Most clients who use private detectives are private citizens who don't think they'll ever need one. They think the police and social services will take care of them. But when they have a problem and don't know how to handle it, the police and social services can be confusing and frustrating. I want my clients to feel confident that they've come to the right place for help.

The other key message I'd like to impart to anyone thinking of starting either their own agency or other business is to always be on the lookout for talent. Try to attract new team members who have the potential or who are already good at their specialist field. Finding a good field agent who can knock on doors and immediately get the public on their side, or a digital technician who can actually do the complicated computer stuff (!) is worth encouraging and holding onto.

Mike Jennings, founder of Cotswold Private Investigations

Refresher Check

'SWOT' analysis is a common tool for identifying the challenges and opportunities ahead. What does 'SWOT' stand for and what does the process involve?

Can you list the six most common business structures and describe each?

When considering how to choose your business name, can you list three of the things you should consider?

A well-crafted business plan should encompass seven key sections. Can you name them and describe each?

For Terms and Conditions what are the three C's?

One common pitfall for new businesses is excessive flexibility in invoicing. Inconsistent payments can lead to cash flow problems, leaving you uncertain and unprepared for unexpected expenses or hindering growth planning. To avoid these pitfalls, it's essential to consider three things. Can you list them?

There are four types of insurance a new business owner should consider when setting up. Can you list them?

SEO is an acronym for what?

Recommended Further Reading

'*Why are Terms and Conditions so Important?*', So Legal (May 2023)

'*How to Start a Small Business*', Federation of Small Businesses (February 2024)

'*Set Up a Business*', www.gov.uk

'*Starting a Business*', www.helptogrow.campaign.gov.uk

'*How to start a small business*', www.business.hsbc.uk

'*How to start a business in 10 steps: a guide for UK entrepreneurs*', Maxine Bremner (December 2023) www.sumup.com

'*Business Advice*', www.kingstrust.org.uk

'*Advice and ideas for small businesses and SMEs*', www.smallbusiness.co.uk

Chapter Two
Client Management

Introduction

Successful businesses can only remain successful by having effective client management. This requires the development of a strong relationship with a client built upon trust, openness and good communication. In this chapter we will look at some effective client management strategies, some obvious do's and don't's as well as considering it from the perspective of the client and the things they should be taking into consideration when deciding whether or not to instruct you in the first place.

Learning Outcomes

By the end of this chapter you will:

- Have a better understanding of what client management is and what the benefits of doing it well can be for your business.
- Know some of the key principles of client management.
- Be aware of the importance of feedback to you both during the investigation and at the conclusion.
- Understand some of the key considerations for those tasked with instructing private investigators, particularly where that is a law firm.

What is Client Management?

Client management is the practice of maintaining a positive relationship with a company's clients. It requires the coordination and management of interactions between a client and the organisation, and has a major impact on a company's reputation and its ability to retain and gain new clients.

When the client feels satisfied, the company is more likely to retain its business. Likewise when the client feels dissatisfied you are unlikely to get repeat business. This aspect of the business should be viewed as an investment rather than as an additional cost. Done well, it will pay dividends.

Client management can be broken down into four distinct parts:
1. Understanding your client's needs and what they want from you.
2. Delivering on those requirements and responding promptly to their questions.
3. Anticipating the needs of the client before they ask for something.
4. Focusing on targeted communications that highlight the needs of the client.

Benefits of Client Management

Client management is important for preserving a good name with the customers, clients and businesses you want business from. A client who is confident in your work will trust you to deliver a professional service. They can perceive your team and business as both credible and professional, one that cares about their expectations.

In the private investigation field, clients are often approaching because they are vulnerable – whether that be from an ongoing divorce or other relationship troubles, family dispute or they are in some other form of legal jeopardy. They are coming to you because they need help and they are prepared to pay for a professional, quality service.

Aside from increasing the likelihood of repeat business from the individual client, getting this bit of your business right can also make it more likely you will attract new clients to your organisation. One satisfied customer is exponentially more likely to refer you to their own network of friends, family and other professional contacts. The more clients you have, the more your business can grow. Whilst you will need to develop a tailored, individual approach to meet the individual needs of each client (unfortunately one size does not fit all!), it is important to recognise those aspects of client management which are common across the board (the generic principles of client management) so you are refining as you go along rather than reinventing every time. This approach will retain the right balance between a bespoke, tailored approach and applying an efficient, corporate process.

Client Management Principles

There are some key principles to help any business build effective client management. Three major principles of client management include:

First Principle: Transparency

Being transparent means being straightforward and honest when interacting with your client. Transparency can help you to avoid misinformation that might lead your client to form an incorrect interpretation of the relationship with your business. You'll also need to make the parameters of the client's instruction to you very clear so both parties understand very clearly from the outset, before you as a professional investigator expend time and resources, exactly what is being asked of you. It is also crucial at this early stage to be clear about whether any evidence acquired during the course of the investigation will likely need to be admissible in court at a later stage of proceedings.

Second Principle: Communication

Being in regular contact with your client will help you be transparent about your progress, or indeed lack of progress. In the latter case this can be particularly important where a lack of progress is for reasons beyond your control and not because you have been inactive or inattentive to the enquiry. Before you start the investigation, confer with your client to decide their preferred method of communication such as email, phone calls or in-person meetings. It's always a good idea to follow up any phone or in-person chats with an email detailing what was covered so that there is a written recap of what was discussed. Consider allowing the client to decide how often you communicate and respond in a timely fashion when they contact you. Here are examples of occasions where it may be necessary to interact with the client:

- **Before the project begins.** You meet the client through video conferencing or in person to discuss the purpose of the project and their ideal results. Thorough communication can also help you to convince clients to choose your business for their needs over competitors. This is an opportunity to highlight any particular strengths of the team in terms of expertise in any given field of investigation.

- **During the project.** The client may request that you give them regular updates about the progress of the investigation. For example, if there is an unforeseen circumstance, such as inclement weather or a shortage of personnel to deploy at the time in question, you can explain how the situation can change deadlines and your efforts to resolve the issue.

- **After you deliver the final product.** At this stage, the client may give your team feedback on the investigation you conducted to help you to improve your approach for the future. Asking for feedback in this way should be something you actively seek and not have 'done to you'. It is an opportunity not a threat.

Third Principle: Alignment

Alignment contributes to the strength of the client-company relationship. It ensures the interests of the client match what the company can deliver. In short, this means are you able to deliver what is being asked of you or not? Do you have the requisite skill set within the team or are you doomed to fail from the start? If the latter, you would be better advised to refer the enquiry on to a more qualified competitor thereby retaining the professional integrity in the eyes of the client (and who would still therefore be a potential future client) as well as building reciprocity with the competitor.

Determine alignment before you agree to a new task, that way you will have complete confidence that your team's skillset and schedule availability can meet the client's expectations.

Client Management Responsibilities

In smaller organisations, client management might be assigned to a specific manager or department. In many companies, a client manager communicates and works with clients. Client managers take part in everything from account planning to client satisfaction surveys. The reality in a small private investigations company is that this will actually be the responsibility of the person at the head of the company – the owner. But as professional investigators working on a contract basis for an investigations company, the principles still apply: the client is the private investigations company. As a freelance investigator working for a company you will want to be re-hired as the work comes in. Here are some tasks that client managers perform regularly:

- Act as the primary connection between the organisation and the client.
- Build relationships with clients and client staff.
- Work with internal teams to help serve clients.
- Identify trends in a client's industry.
- Find patterns in client feedback through satisfaction surveys.
- Anticipate challenges and assess risks for projects.
- Guide clients on purchasing decisions.
- Find opportunities for new work.

Client Management Best Practices

To build a client management technique, follow these five steps:

1. **Understand the needs of the client.** The initial step to meeting the client's objectives is to understand what they envisage for the final product. During your first meeting, be transparent when discussing how the client's expectations align with your team's capabilities. Learn what your client wants to achieve as a result of the product or service you're offering.

2. **Create a clear outline.** Determine the steps your team will take to complete the project by outlining your detailed strategy for accomplishing the client's goal. An outline can include a timeline of when you plan to start the project and when you expect to deliver it, which you can use to negotiate your deadlines with the client. Having a clear outline can show your preparedness for launching a project and organisational skills. As a private investigator, this would typically be defined as an investigation plan.

3. **Update the client on progress.** It's essential to keep the client informed about your progress on the assignment. Reserve time at consistent intervals to speak with the client directly about what you've accomplished so far and what's next on the agenda. The frequency of your updates can depend on the client's interests and the complexity of your project. Regular updates about your progress can show your dedication to meeting their needs and you can maintain their confidence in the productivity of your team. For example, if the investigation lasts several months, you might decide to schedule a meeting with the client once every two weeks to explain your progress, or you can send a message after you've completed an agreed milestone. Agree a joint schedule.

4. **Document every step of the project.** Documentation refers to records of every task you complete for the client. Records can help you to avoid discrepancies between your work and your client agreement. Consider documenting the dates of when you began the assignment along with challenges you faced and changes you've made as you've progressed. Your notes can provide a reference of what you've achieved so far, which can be helpful if your assignment is extensive. You'll also create records you can review later when you take on similar projects. We will return to the issue of record keeping in the final chapter.

5. **Apply the client's feedback.** As you make progress on your investigation, the client might offer constructive criticism on how to improve your work. Applying their feedback can illustrate your commitment to delivering a product that meets their needs. Ask questions to gain clarification on what the client wants and develop strategies with your team on ways to achieve their vision. If the client issues feedback after the completion of the project, you can record their feedback to fulfil future requests. This becomes more challenging when the client is making well-intentioned suggestions motivated by their needs but which are in conflict with other desired outcomes, for example, the requirement for any evidential material obtained during the course of the investigation to be admissible in court.

Client Management Pitfalls to Avoid

Here are common pitfalls to avoid when learning how to manage clients:

- **Not prioritising clients.** While you may feel pressure to constantly bring in new clients, it's important to prioritise existing clients. If you don't schedule time to attend to your current clients, you risk missing opportunities to upsell or your clients leaving for competitors who make cheap promises.
- **Not listening to clients' needs.** Client managers who try to sell clients new services or products without making meaningful connections won't be able to develop lasting relationships. Listen to your clients' goals and what they actually need.
- **Not being organised.** Keep everyone in your organisation updated on each client by using a client relationship management (CRM) system. In the absence of a bespoke system, regular in-person team meetings can be just as effective where all ongoing cases and options are discussed in an open forum. Colleagues should, as far as is appropriate, know the status of a current project, goals and all recent communications for every client. This can pay dividends for ensuring continuity of investigations where a team member is lost as a deployable resource through illness, for example.

Considerations by Clients

We have looked in depth at strategies and tips from the perspective of the professional private investigator but it would also be helpful to consider the same question from the other side of the equation. What are the considerations for those actually tasked with instructing a private investigator? Particularly where there is no pre-existing professional relationship? This list is by no means exhaustive but includes the following:

- Ensure there is credible independent accountability to a professional body.
- Ask about their data protection training. Are they registered with the Information Commissioner's Office?
- Question their level of professional indemnity insurance to ensure that it meets the maximum exposure should anything go wrong.
- Insist any proposal is in writing, that it addresses the lawful basis to meet the task and that their methods are clear, compliant and meet your expectations.

Where the instruction is coming from a law firm, either directly or on behalf of a private client, be aware that they will have additional considerations in order to remain compliant with their own professional regulatory bodies. Considerations for law firms include the following:

- They must ensure they are acting in their client's best interests and on their instructions.
- Carrying out full due diligence on the private investigation company and those that will be providing the service. Avoid just relying on references as the firms providing them may not have done sufficient due diligence themselves.
- Ask if the company is ISO registered or holds any formal accreditations. (ISO stands for the International Organisation of Standardisation.)
- Ask if all staff have a current CRB check and receive regular training.
- Undertake a web search of the company and see if they come up in any negative context.
- Review the performance of the private investigator on an ongoing basis – they are acting on your instructions so you can be liable for what they do.

A very useful article about instructing private investigators appeared in the Law Society Gazette in March 2014 and is well worth a read, especially as one of the investigators interviewed said, *"There are some real sharks out there who can be totally convincing, but who will take your money without doing the job. They will obtain data illegally, which could rebound on the reputation of the law firm and its client, and cost you fines. They will also frequently provide information that is inadmissible as evidence in a court of law and so waste your money if you paid them to get it.".*

Law firms instructing private investigators need to assess their exposure to the regulations and their current obligations under the Solicitor's Regulatory Handbook. Clearly this area poses real risks and therefore the firms involved should consider placing the issue in their risk register. As a private investigator, being aware of these considerations by those potentially instructing you will help you to address those issues before they are even posed.

Examples of Client Testimonials Received

"...After taking the plunge and contacting Cotswold Private Investigations I knew I was in good hands from the start. After months of denial from my partner (of 20 years), I was beginning to doubt my sanity. I knew something was happening and Cotswold Private Investigations helped me find the truth. They also supported me when the time was right to confront my husband and helped me prepare for that moment so the power was in my hands and I was in control. I am happy to recommend their services and if like me you think you're losing your marbles I would encourage you to give them a call."

"As the owner of a small distribution business, we were experiencing a higher than normal loss and breakages ratio which, to some extent is to be expected but we were starting to notice an upward trend. After contacting Cotswold Private Investigations they advised us on a course of action which (without going into detail here) allowed us to arrest this trend and bring the human factor that was contributing towards this back under control. Unfortunately, this meant losing the individual at the centre (and influencing others) but with the evidential reports supplied by Cotswold Private Investigations, we were able to navigate the process smoothly and fairly without the need of a costly tribunal. Once presented with the evidence the individual at the centre decided to resign. Cotswold Private Investigations helped save us the considerable extra cost in both HR and legal fees as well as lost revenue through damage and loss which had it continued might even have cost us repeat client business."

"(long story short)...Cotswold Private Investigations helped me find out the truth that my husband was being unfaithful (with one of my best friends) and with the help of my Case Manager (thanks Lynn) helped me find a good solicitor, removal company to move me back to my parents and closer to my support network and even a change of school for the children. Throughout the whole awful process, I felt supported and never alone. So when you contacted me and asked me to write this review I was more than happy to do so and recommend to others your professional services. Thank you for helping me to get my life (and self-respect) back."

"...the feeling of not knowing and being lied to was awful. Cotswold Private Investigations stopped this and gave me the answers I needed within days of first contacting them. Thank you, Capt. Mike and the rest of the team."

Refresher Check

What are the four distinct parts of client management? What are the three principles of client management?

There are five steps of successful client management best practice discussed in this chapter. Can you name three of them?

Can you describe two of the three client management pitfalls to avoid?

List four things a law firm may need to consider when deciding whether or not to instruct a private investigation firm.

Recommended Further Reading

'*Client Management: A Complete Guide with Tips*', Indeed (2024)

'*Private Investigators – checks you make when instructing them*', Rogers (2014)

'*Instructing Investigators and Process Servers*', The Law Society (2019)

'*How Clients Buy: A Practical Guide to Business Development for Consulting and Professional Services*', Tom McMakin (2018)

'*The Art of Client Service*', Robert Solomon (2008) '*People Buy You*', Jon Blount (2010)

'*5 Star Service: How to Deliver Exceptional Customer Service*', Michael Heppell (2015)

'*Tips and Best Practices for Mastering Client Management*', Diana Ramos (June 2023)

'*Ready to Master Client Management? Here's How!*', Erdem (April 2024)

'*The Importance of Client Management*', Robert Walters (December 2022)

'*Client Management 101: strategies to build strong client relationships*', Tejasvini Ramesh (April 2022)

'*10 Best Practices for Client Relationship Management*', Jeffrey Kagan (October 2024)

'*How to Surpass Customers' Expectations: Building Solid Client Relationships*', Adam Tau (January 2023)

Chapter Three
Invoicing

Introduction

We touched on this important issue briefly in Chapter One but it is an important enough aspect of running a successful business to warrant more in-depth study. Running a business comes with a lot of responsibilities – one of the most crucial being invoicing. As well as making sure we get paid, invoices serve other important purposes, some of which might not be immediately obvious.

Having the correct documentation with the payment terms in writing can offer a level of legal protection, as it provides a record of your agreed services. Invoices act as a marker of your professionalism, helping to demonstrate that you're a business your clients can trust.

For businesses of all sizes throughout the UK, invoicing is a fundamental part of maintaining healthy cash flow and ensuring that services and products are paid for on time. A clear and professional invoice not only helps in getting paid promptly but also ensures compliance with UK regulations. To help you to ensure that your invoices are in tip top shape we will now look at some useful tips for creating and managing invoices efficiently.

Learning Outcomes

By the end of this section you will:

- Have a better understanding of the important details to include in your invoices.
- Be able to apply some best practice principles to your invoicing.
- Consider going the extra mile to distinguish yourself from others by personalising your invoices.

What is the Difference Between Invoicing and Billing?

The main difference between invoicing and billing is the level of detail and the timing of the payment. Invoices provide more detailed information, including payment terms and client details. Invoices are often used in business-to-business transactions, and can be issued before or after the client receives the goods or services. Invoices are legally binding and can be used to request payment before a pre-approved date.

Bills provide less detailed information and are usually paid for immediately or within a short time frame. Bills are more common in business-to-client transactions such as when you receive a bill from a restaurant or a car mechanic.

What Should be Included in an Invoice?

To ensure your invoices are clear, professional and legally compliant, they must include the following crucial elements:

- **Your business's information.** Your business name, address and contact details; your company registration number (if you are a limited company) and/or VAT number.
- **Your client's information.** The full name and address of the client or customer being invoiced.
- **A unique invoice number.** Each invoice should have a unique reference number for your business's tracking purposes. This is particularly important for bookkeeping and when dealing with any potential disputes.
- **An invoice date.** The date the invoice is issued to the client. This will allow them to track when payment is due.
- **A clear description of the goods or service you supplied/ provided.** This should include dates, quantity or hours worked if applicable, as well as a clear description of what was provided. Clients don't want to be presented with a document filled with items or figures and being unable to make immediate sense of it. Making sure your invoices are clear makes it easier to get paid and maintain a good ongoing relationship with your clients. You can ask yourself some simple questions to ensure your invoices are supporting you:

- How simple is it to locate information such as reference numbers, descriptions of items, and, importantly, the payment terms on your invoices?
- Have I used over-complicated language or abbreviations that could cause confusion? Never take for granted that a customer will know what is meant by these terms. Just because you are familiar with TLAs (three letter abbreviations) or acronyms does not mean your clients will be.
- Overall, have I kept it simple and concise to get across the important points without the need for additional clarification?

- **The total amount due.** Relevant charges should be broken down for each product or service as follows:
  - **Net amount.** The total cost before any taxes.
  - **VAT (if applicable).** For VAT-registered businesses, the VAT amount should be clearly displayed.
  - **Gross amount.** The total amount including VAT.
- **Agreed payment terms.** You should include the payment terms that were previously agreed with your client, for example, thirty days from date of invoices, as well as details for any penalties for late payments. Equally, however don't leave it to the client to chase invoices. This puts them in an awkward situation that could easily be avoided. Paying people on time, or early even, strengthens relationships, builds trust and can eliminate late fees, so it's worth making sure invoices are a thought-through part of your purchase flow.
- **Details on how to pay.** You will need to detail precisely how your client can pay you. Clearly outline your bank details.
- **Contact details.** Make it as easy as possible for your client to contact your business should they have a query regarding an invoice.

Invoicing Best Practice

Aside from ensuring your invoice is accurately raised and sent to a client, here are a few tips on how to ensure you can maintain positive cash flow through invoicing best practice:

- **Send invoices promptly.** Delayed invoicing can lead to delayed payments. Ensure invoices are sent out as soon as the service or product is delivered.

- **Use professional invoicing software.** Your chosen accounting software can automate and streamline the invoicing process, including generating invoices, tracking payments and maintaining accurate records.
- **Follow-up on overdue payments.** Client-focused credit control is a must when it comes to invoicing.
- **Maintain accurate records.** Keep copies of all invoices for your records, whether digital or paper. This will prove key for accounting purposes, not to mention when it comes to your self-assessment tax returns.

Ultimately, invoicing is a vital part of running any business. By ensuring your invoices are clear, professional and compliant with UK regulations, you will maintain good cash flow and build positive relationships with clients.

Everybody likes to feel appreciated and invoices represent a great opportunity to show gratitude to your clients for their business. Making clients feel recognised is one of the best ways to build a strong relationship and trust – something that can play an important role if you want them to come back to you with more business. Adding a short, personalised thank you message is also a chance to add some personality on your invoice and show that you are distinctive and more than just an anonymous entity.

Exercise

You are a sole trader not registered for VAT. On 15/06/25 you took a case from a client involved in a matrimonial dispute who wanted you to follow her spouse. Accordingly on 20/06/25 you spent two hours following the subject, on 21/06/25 you spent a further three hours following the subject and lastly a further three hours on 22/06/25 before your client terminated the case and asked to be invoiced for the costs incurred to date.

Your hourly rate is £40 for this type of work.

Using a blank template create an invoice to send to the client.

Note – for the purposes of this exercise you may create your own customer identity as well as your own business name and other details. Also assume there were no incidental expenses incurred.

COTSWOLD
Private Investigations

Addressee:	Joe Bloggs	Invoice #:	Invoice Reference
Email:	joebloggs@gmail.com	Date:	1 January 2025

Invoice

Description		Cost (GBP)
Deposit for investigative services		425.00
	VAT 20%	85.00
	Total to Pay	**510.00**

Payment Terms: Immediate, due upon receipt of invoice
Payment Reference: Please use surname

DIRECT ALL INVOICE ENQUIRIES TO

Name: Invoice Contact Name
Phone: Office Telephone Number
Email: name@companyname.co.uk

PAYABLE TO

Name: COTSWOLD PRIVATE INVESTIGATIONS LTD
Account #: 00000000
Sort Code: 00-00-00
Bank: Bank
SWIFT BIC: MYMBGB3M
IBAN: GB33MYMB00000000000000

Thank You!
Registered address:

Example of a Deposit Invoice

Addressee:	Joe Bloggs	Invoice #:	Invoice Reference
	joebloggs@gmail.com	Date:	1 January 2025

Date	Description	Agent	Hours Worked (GBP 85/hour)	Cost (GBP)
01/01	OFFICE – pre-deployment planning (tracker and surveillance	James	2 hours	170.00
01/01	OFFICE – consultation	John	3.5 hours	297.50
01/01	MILEAGE – 81 miles @ 45p/mile			36.45
03/01	FIELD – tracker deployment (1st attempt)	Joe	3.5 hours	297.50
03/01	MILEAGE – 120 miles @ 45p/mile	Joe		54.00
04/01	FIELD – tracker deployment (2nd attempt), tracker fitted	Joe	3.5 hours	297.50
04/01	MILEAGE – 120 miles @ 45p/mile	Joe		54.00
04/01	TRACKER – 1 week usage (£35/day)			245.00
06/01	FIELD – surveillance day (2 agents, 7 hours each)	Joe, John	14 hours	1,190.00
06/01	MILEAGE – 160 miles @ 45p/mile	Joe		72.00
11/01	FIELD – tracker removal	Joe	3.5 hours	297.50
11/01	MILEAGE – 120 miles @ 45p/mile	Joe		54.00
	OFFICE – post-deployment video editing and report writing	Joe	1.5 hours	127.50
	OSINT – background research and target report			500.00
	Database fees			85.00
			Subtotal	3,777.95
			VAT 20%	755.59
			Subtotal	4,533.54
			Minus deposit paid	-510.00
			Total to Pay	4,023.54

Payment Terms: Immediate, due upon receipt of invoice
Payment Reference: Please use surname

DIRECT ALL INVOICE ENQUIRIES TO
Name: Invoice Contact Name
Phone: Office Telephone Number
Email: name@companyname.co.uk

PAYABLE TO
Name: COTSWOLD PRIVATE INVESTIGATIONS LTD
Account #: 00000000
Sort Code: 00-00-00
Bank: Bank
SWIFT BIC: MYMBGB3M
IBAN: GB33MYMB00000000000000

Example of a Detailed Invoice

Refresher Check

If VAT is applicable this does not need to be shown on your invoices, it is for the client to add. True or false?

Payment terms are always non-negotiable and are determined by the provider and not the client. True or false?

Don't risk aggravating your client by chasing overdue payments as this might just annoy them. Be patient and wait until they pay. True or false?

Recommended Further Reading

https://www.gov.uk/invoicing-and-taking-payment-from-customers/invoices-what-they-must-include

https://www.gov.uk/guidance/electronic-invoicing-notice-70063

https://www.gov.uk/government/publications/invoicing-customers-oisc-practice-note/invoicing- customers

'*Invoicing: a best practice checklist*', Sufio Professional Invoices (2021)

'*A Basic Guide to Invoicing*', Ellis + Co Chartered Accountants (2024)

'*Invoice Book Self-Employed: Invoicing Made Easy for Self-Employed A Guide and Log Book*', Aaliyah (2023)

'*Easy Steps to Invoicing and Follow Up*', Alison Reid (August 2020)

'*Invoicing for Creatives – Get Paid in Full and On Time*', Gavin Ricketts (September 2013)

'*Electronic Invoicing – A Clear and Concise Reference*', Gerardus Blokdyk (June 2018)

Chapter Four
Process Serving

Introduction

Process serving in England and Wales is the act of delivering legal documents to individuals or organisations as an integral part of the legal process. The most common type of legal documents to be served include summonses, complaints, subpoenas, insolvency demands and proceedings, court orders, common law notices, divorce petitions, bankruptcy and winding up petitions and family proceedings. The process server is responsible for ensuring that the documents are delivered to the correct recipient in a timely and professional manner.

Process serving is an important part of the legal system in England and Wales, as it ensures that individuals and organisations are notified of legal proceedings and have the opportunity to respond in a timely and professional manner. Process serving is an integral task for any individual involved in private investigations and it is important to understand what your role is, as well as its limitations.

Learning Outcomes

By the end of this section you will:

- Understand the importance of Part 6 of the Civil Procedure Rules as well as some of the key elements including methods of service, types of acceptable service and important dates to be aware of.
- Understand the importance of a Particulars of Claim and Certificates of Service.
- Be aware of some different scenarios for service and your responsibilities as a professional investigator.

The Civil Procedure Rules (Part 6)

Before going any further it is important to consider the overarching legislation which governs this important area of activity. The Civil Procedure Rules (henceforth referred to as 'the rules' or CPR) Part 6 specifically deals with the service of documents, outlining the procedures and requirements for ensuring that parties in litigation receive the necessary legal documents.

What is CPR Part 6?

CPR Part 6 sets out the rules for the service of documents in civil proceedings. Service is the process of formally delivering legal documents to the relevant parties, ensuring that they are informed of the proceedings and have an opportunity to respond. We will now look at the key provisions of Part 6 of the rules broken down by the relevant sections.

Methods of Service (CPR 6.3)

CPR 6.3 specifies the various methods by which documents can be served, including:

- **Personal service.** Delivering documents directly to the individual.
- **First class post.** Sending documents via first class post.
- **Electronic service.** Serving documents via email or other electronic means, where agreed or permitted.
- **Leaving at an address.** Leaving documents at the individual's address.

Service Within the Jurisdiction (CPR 6.4-6.7)

These provisions outline the rules for serving documents within England and Wales, including:

- **Service by the court.** The court may serve documents on behalf of a party.
- **Service on individuals and companies.** Specific rules for serving individuals, companies, partnerships and other entities.

Service Outside the Jurisdiction (CPR 6.40-6.47)

CPR 6.40-6.47 cover the rules for serving documents outside of England and Wales. These include:

- **International service.** Procedures for serving documents in foreign countries.
- **Service in convention countries.** Special rules for countries that are parties to international conventions on service.

Deemed Service (CPR 6.14)

CPR 6.14 outlines the rules for deemed service, which is the assumption that service has been effected after a certain period, depending on the method of service used.

Importance of CPR Part 6

Ensuring Due Process

CPR Part 6 ensures that all parties receive the necessary legal documents, which is essential for upholding the principles of due process. Proper service guarantees that parties are aware of the proceedings and have an opportunity to respond.

Promoting Fairness

By outlining clear rules for the service of documents, CPR Part 6 promotes fairness in the litigation process. It ensures that no party is disadvantaged by not receiving critical legal documents in a timely manner.

Enhancing Efficiency

Standardised procedures for serving documents enhance the efficiency of the litigation process. Proper service avoids delays and ensures that cases proceed smoothly through the court system.

Practical Implications for Litigants and Legal Professionals

Understanding and complying with CPR Part 6 is crucial for anyone involved in civil litigation. Legal professionals must ensure that documents are served correctly to avoid potential issues in the case.

Tips for Compliance

- **Choose the appropriate method.** Select the most appropriate method of service based on the circumstances and the rules outlined in CPR Part 6.
- **Follow protocols for international service.** Be aware of the specific requirements for serving documents outside of the jurisdiction.
- **Adhere to timeframes.** Ensure that documents are served within the specified timeframes to comply with court deadlines.

- **Maintain records.** Keep detailed records of all service attempts and methods used to provide proof of service if required.

In conclusions, CPR Part 6 plays a critical role in the civil litigation process by regulating the service of documents. Proper service is crucial in litigation. We will now consider some of these areas in more detail.

What is it that Can be Served?

Under the rules, a document that can be served includes any claim form, application notice, order, judgment or other legal document filed with or sent by the court. The requirements for service of a claim form are treated separately from other legal documents because this form, along with the Particulars of Claim, initiates the entire litigation process. Without a claim form service, time does not start in the proceedings for other events in the litigation case such as when a default judgment may be applied for or when defences or counterclaims are due. In other words, without a claim form, legal proceedings cannot begin.

Particulars of Claim

The Particulars of Claim (sometimes referred to as 'pleadings') are a concise statement of the grounds upon which the claimant's case is based. The claimant is the party bringing a claim to court. The claimant form will often contain the Particulars. However, they may be sometimes seen in a separate document altogether.

The purpose of the Particulars of Claim is to inform the defendant of the case and what they have to defend at its early stages. As such, the Particulars of Claim will set out the facts that constitute the causes of action. The causes of action refer to the fact or facts that enable the claimant to bring an action against the defendant. The claimant must state all of the facts that are necessary to form the complete cause of action against the defendant. They must also give the defendant enough information for them to understand the case the claimant is bringing against them. In addition, the Particulars of Claim must set out the remedies being sought.

Why Might a Particulars of Claim be Inadequate?

If the Particulars of Claim is inadequate a court can strike out the claim altogether. There are several reasons why it might prove inadequate:

- The claimant is so unclear that the defendants cannot reasonably be expected to understand the case against them.

- The defendant has to incur unreasonable expenses to respond to the allegations because the claim is not clear enough.
- If the courts will be unsure what they are being asked to decide.
- If a claim is understandable but lacks the required amount of detail, a court may require amendment or clarification rather than completely striking the claim.

What Should a Particulars of Claim Include?

- Identity of the parties, including their full, unabbreviated name.
- Causes of action.
- Remedies being sought (although it is important to note also that the court may give any remedy it deems appropriate even if it is not requested in the claims form).
- Interest calculations as part of the claim.
- Material facts of any allegations.
- Alternative possibilities of facts.
- Loss and damage the claimant has allegedly suffered.

Responding to a Particulars of Claim

A response to a Particulars of Claim should include:

- Whether the allegations being made are admitted to, denied or proof is sought before responding.
- Any alternative version of events making up the defendant's case (rebuttal).
- The structure of the defence.
- Reasons for ending specific allegations.
- Personal information including full name, address and date of birth.
- Any suggestion that a limitation period has been breached, meaning the claimant is time-barred from even bringing such a claim.
- Any defences of contributory negligence, illegality or failure to mitigate loss.

In short, both parties are disclosing to each other the grounds of their case and the evidence they will rely on for making it.

As a professional investigator if you are involved in the service of a Particulars of Claim or you are being served, you should seek legal advice.

Who Can Serve?

Documents may be served by the court directly or a party to the case, as well as various officials like bailiffs or sheriffs. Parties can also instruct process servers – third-party individuals or businesses certified to serve documents on a claimant's behalf.

How to Serve

Serving documents on the other parties of a dispute is a critical early stage in any claim. By serving the documents, the other party has been made fully aware of the details of the claim by receiving all of the papers in the case. Common methods of service include the following:

- Personal service under Civil Procedure Rule Part 6.5 (handing the document to the recipient directly or a senior representative within a company).
- First class post, official document exchange or another next business day service.
- Delivery of the document to or leaving the document in a specified place.
- Fax or other electronic means, where agreed.
- Any method authorised by the court in Rule 6.15.

Contrary to widespread belief, email is not adequate to initiate the service of documents. Under Part 6, Rule 23 of the CPR, it's stipulated that, *"Where a party indicates in accordance with Practice Direction 6A that they will accept service by electronic means other than fax, the email address or electronic identification given by that party will be deemed to be at the address for service."*.

Practice Direction 6A, paragraph 4.1 states, "…*where a document is to be served by fax or other electronic means the party who is to be served or the solicitor acting for that party must previously have indicated in writing to the party serving:*

- *That the party to be served or the solicitor is willing to accept service by fax.*
- *That the party to be served or the solicitor is willing to accept service by fax or other electronic means; and*
- *The fax number, email address or other electronic identification to which it must be sent."*.

Furthermore, Practice Direction 6, paragraph 4.2 states that,"*Where a party intends to serve a document by electronic means (other than by fax) that party must first ask the party who is to be served whether there are any limitations to the recipient's agreement to accept service by such means (for example, the format in which documents are to be sent and the maximum size of attachments that may be received).*". Under Part 6, Rule 9 of the CPR, none of the places at which individuals may be served refer to email.

What if the Party to be Served is Overseas?

If an overseas party needs to be served, the process varies by which country they are located in. Special permission and authorisation from a court is required to serve documents that fall outside English court authority. An Application Notice is required, by which point, relevant international laws may govern how service can take place.

Serving Documents Upon Solicitors

Solicitors may be authorised to accept service on behalf of a party in the absence of direct communication to the claimant. A claim form must be served at the business address of that solicitor. Subject to Rule 6.5(1) where the party has given in writing the business address within a solicitor's jurisdiction, or a solicitor acting for the party has notified the claimant (in writing) of their authorisation to accept service.

Other Scenarios

If you wish to serve notice for a contractual dispute, your contract will probably dictate where you have to serve notice to. This can occasionally also feature in property contracts.

If you wish to serve documents on a defendant but do not have an address for them, you can serve on an individual by sending the notice to their usual or last known residence.

For a company registered in England and Wales, you can serve documents by sending them to the principal office of the company, or any place of business of the company in England and Wales which has a real connection with the claim. For example, if you have a claim against a supermarket for an accident that happened in one of their stores, you could serve on the supermarket HQ or the individual store where the accident happened.

Important Dates

The purpose of service is to bring a claim form or other document to the attention of another party. The rules mandate that a specific point in time be stated, as time runs for further steps to be taken in proceedings from that point.

The date of service is the point in time for other events. These include:

- fixing a date to calculate limitations periods
- when service acknowledgements are due to be filed
- when default judgments, defences or counterclaims may be filed
- sanctions and relief from applications running from specific dates.

It is critical to know the precise date of service, since deadlines for response often run from that, not when documents were produced, and could impact case timelines and outcomes. The date a document is considered served is not necessarily the date that it was posted or sent. In-person delivery effectively serves documents on the day that action takes place, whereas other channels may indicate a difference in the document creation date and the actual service date.

Challenges to Service

A party has the option to contest service if they believe the rules have not been properly followed. If the court agrees, this may invalidate service and the document(s) being served would need to be served again. Disputes might relate to the method and timing of service or the information provided alongside documents.

While technical, understanding the rules (particularly in the context of Part 6) is vital for accurately serving and challenging documents in litigation and ensures cases proceed fairly and efficiently through the justice system.

Certificates of Service

A Certificate of Service is a formal document that informs the court that a party has served a document on another party. It is used to provide evidence that documents were served on time and properly, which allows the court to proceed with the relevant proceedings.

A Certificate of Service is required when the claimant serves the claim form on the defendant, rather than the court. It is specific to the claim form and must be verified by a Statement of Truth and include the following information:

- The documents served.
- Who the documents were served on.
- When, where and how the documents were served.
- A statement that the document has not been returned undelivered.

The Certificate of Service is usually completed using Court Form N215, which is only suitable for claims in England and Wales. It is important to ensure that all details are accurate before signing the form, as failure to do so could have serious legal consequences.

Scenario: Evasive Debtors

The tasking was to serve court papers to a married couple, Mr and Mrs X, who owed over £50,000 to a creditor, our client. The couple had evaded multiple attempts by other servers, changing addresses frequently and using aliases. We began by cross-referencing public records, utility databases and social media activity. This showed us that the couple had recently rented a property in Southampton under false names. Surveillance revealed they rarely left home during daylight hours, complicating direct contact.

The Serve Attempt

Very early one morning two colleagues positioned themselves near the property. When Mr X stepped outside to collect a delivery, we approached calmly, identified ourselves and handed over the documents. Mr X became hostile, slamming the door. Undeterred, we returned that evening, catching Mrs X as she arrived home. She initially denied her identity but relented when she was presented with photographic evidence. However, she refused to accept the papers, prompting us to place them at her feet – a legally valid method under UK law. To ensure compliance, we filed an affidavit detailing the time, location and manner of service, including our own witness statements. The court accepted this proof, allowing the creditor's case to proceed.

Lessons Learned

Persistence and Adaptability

Evasive targets require creative strategies. We combined digital tracing with physical surveillance, adapting this approach when initial attempts failed. This aligns with the need for all professional investigators to be resourceful and able to adapt to changing circumstances.

Legal Precision Matters

Documenting every interaction meticulously ensured validity. As highlighted in process serving guidelines, incomplete proof of service can derail cases.

Respectful Engagement

Despite hostility, we maintained professionalism. Treating respondents respectfully, even when met with aggression, prevented escalation and built cooperation.

Team Coordination

Use of a colleague as a witness underscores the value of teamwork, especially for high-stakes serves. Coordinated efforts, like those in multi-location serves, ensure compliance with tight deadlines.

Ethical Boundaries

We avoided trespassing or confrontational tactics, adhering to UK laws. Overstepping the law risks invalidating service and damaging credibility.

Conclusion

This scenario illustrates how UK private investigators blend investigative rigour with legal expertise to navigate complex serves. By prioritising persistence, ethical conduct and thorough documentation, they uphold judicial integrity while overcoming evasion tactics. As the field evolves, embracing technology and continuous learning remains critical.

Refresher Check

What are the Particulars of Claim?

What is a cause of action?

List three acceptable ways of service.

The date by which a document is deemed to be served is the date it was posted. True or false?

A Certificate of Service must include what information?

Recommended Further Reading

Serving Documents in the UK: a brief guide', George IDE LLP Solicitors (February 2024)

The right (and wrong) way to serve court documents', Burnetts (2021)

'Litigation Brief: An Overview of CPR Part 6 – Service of Documents', AI Law (July 2024)

'What are the Particulars of a Claim in the UK?', LegalVision (July 2024)

Chapter Five
Report Writing

Introduction

As a private investigator in the UK, a good report to a client should be clear, concise, professional and tailored to their needs. It should provide all relevant information in a structured format while maintaining confidentiality and adhering to legal and ethical standards.

The quality and content of such reports not only serves as a testament to the quality of the service provided, and by implication the quality of the investigation itself, but also reflects upon the professionalism of the company in any subsequent court proceedings through the disclosure process. In this chapter we will look at the various elements which comprise a high-quality, professional client report.

Learning Outcomes

By the end of this section you will:

- Have a good understanding of the various elements of a professional investigator's report to a client.
- Understand why these elements are important.

Title Page

As with any document the first page should always be the title page. This is an opportunity to create a professional tone with the company logo in a prominent position and any branding considerations regarding font and layout applied (see Chapter One on Starting Your Business). A good title page will comprise the following:

- **Title of the report.** Clearly state the purpose of the report, for example, 'Surveillance Report on [Subject Name]'.
- **Client's name.** Include the name of the client or the company you are reporting to.
- **Date of submission.** The date the report is delivered.

- **Case reference number.** If applicable, include a unique identifier for the case.
- **Private investigator's details.** Your name and formal titles or qualifications, and contact information.

Executive Summary

The executive summary is important not only for the obvious reason that it distills what may be a lengthy investigation report into a more manageable summary but also it may be the only part of the report some clients will actually read! Many clients, particularly professional business clients, will turn to this section first so it should always be readily located at the front of the overall report. The executive summary will comprise a brief overview of the investigation, including:
- The purpose of the investigation.
- Key findings or outcomes.
- Any immediate actions or recommendations.

This section should be concise and allow the client to quickly understand the main points. If at all possible, it should consist of no more than one side of A4.

Introduction

The introduction is the start of the main body of the report and should comprise the following elements:
- **Background information.** Explain why the investigation was initiated and the client's objectives.
- **Scope of work.** Outline what was agreed upon, for example, surveillance, background checks, contact with potential witnesses known to the client.
- **Legal compliance.** Briefly state that the investigation was conducted within the bounds of UK law, including adherence to the Data Protection Act 2018, the General Data Protection Regulation and other relevant regulations.

Methodology

In this section of the report you will describe the methods and tools used during the investigation. For example, surveillance, interviews and online research. Ensure transparency while avoiding unnecessary technical jargon and include details such as:

- Dates and times of surveillance.
- Locations visited.
- Equipment used, for example, cameras, GPS trackers.

Findings

From the client's perspective this will be an important part of the report. Clearly if they were motivated to instruct you in the first place they will want to see what findings were reached. These will have been already covered in a verbal report to the client. That said, seeing the findings of a professional investigation laid out in black and white for the first time is an important part of the client/investigator relationship. Ensure that you present the evidence and information gathered in a clear, logical and chronological order. Use headings and subheadings to organise the content, for example, 'Surveillance on [Date]'. Also you should include:

- Detailed observations.
- Photographs, videos or audio recordings (if applicable and legally obtained).
- Witness statements or interview summaries.
- Any relevant documents or records.

Be factual and avoid speculation or personal opinions.

Analysis

This is the 'value added' part of any report where your skills, based upon your knowledge and experience, can provide useful insight into the findings and possible future courses of action the client may wish to consider. This can be particularly important where you are raising the possibility of either further action or, just as importantly, no further action. This section should include the following:

- Your interpretations of the findings in the context of the client's objectives.
- Highlighted patterns, inconsistencies or significant events.
- If applicable, provide a professional assessment of the subject's behaviour or activities.

Conclusion

In essence this is a more detailed version of the executive summary but nonetheless an important element where the extra detail may be useful in explaining how and why any investigation arrived at the outcome it did, good or bad. In this section you should:
- Summarise the key points of the investigation.
- State whether the objectives were met or if further investigation is required.
- Avoid making assumptions or drawing conclusions that are not supported by the evidence.

Recommendations

As with analysis, this is an opportunity for you as the professional investigator to provide your 'value added' insight and comments which, demonstrates to the client the value of the service you have provided. You should be honest and, whilst always mindful of the client's objectives laid out at the commencement of the investigation, not be afraid to recommend a course of action the client may not wish to hear. You should:
- Provide actionable advice based on the findings, for example, legal action, further investigation or no further action required.
- Be clear and practical in your suggestions.

Appendices

Depending upon the nature of the investigation and the report, appendices may or may not be applicable. However, where they can be included they are a valuable addition to providing a sense of completeness and thoroughness to the overall investigation and therefore the quality of the service you have provided to the client. You should include any supporting documents such as:
- Photographs or video stills.
- Maps or diagrams.
- Transcripts of interviews or conversations.
- Copies of relevant records or documents.

Confidentiality Statement

This is another important, albeit brief, element of any report as it demonstrates professionalism on your part and the integrity of the service you are providing to the client. In this section you should reiterate that the report is confidential and intended solely for the client's use. Include a disclaimer stating that the report should not be shared with third parties without your consent.

Sign-Off

This comprises of your name, signature (if submitting a hard copy) and contact details as well as a statement confirming the accuracy and completeness of the report to the best of your knowledge.

Summary of Key Tips for a Professional Report

Clarity. Use plain language and avoid jargon.

Accuracy. Ensure all facts are correct and supported by evidence.

Objectivity. Remain neutral and avoid emotional language.

Formatting. Use a professional font, consistent headings and numbered pages.

Confidentiality. Protect the privacy of all parties involved.

Legal compliance. Ensure all evidence was obtained legally and ethically.

Refresher Check

Can you list three of the elements which comprise a good title page?

The executive summary should provide a brief overview of the investigation as well as three other elements. What are they?

List some of the documents that could be included as Appendices where appropriate?

There are six elements which comprise key tips for a professional report. Can you name them?

Recommended Further Reading

'*How to Write a Report for Work (With Examples)*', Jennifer Herrity for Indeed, (January 2025)

'*Report Writing: Overview*', University of Westminster (2023)

'*How to Write a Great Report: Top Tips for Success*', Oxbridge Essays (October 2024)

Chapter Six
Interviewing Witnesses

Introduction

Interviewing witnesses is one of the core tasks of the professional private investigator. Having a well-grounded approach is key to ensuring that the maximum information and intelligence is gleaned from the interviewee in such a way as the finished product is not only relevant to the investigative objectives but also of evidential quality should it be required at a later court hearing.

However, as with any interaction with a member of the public, particularly one who may be vulnerable, the interview can be both a complex and sensitive process. A successful interview will demand of the investigator not only skilful application of the techniques looked at in this chapter but also sensitivity and the ability to recognise what is relevant information and what is not depending upon the points to prove.

The twin pillars of any effective interview technique are the application of active listening skills combined with use of the PEACE model. In this chapter we will look at each in turn. Many of the techniques and approaches discussed will be the same as for taking witness statements – taking a statement from a witness is essentially an interview except you are writing their account for them, in the first person.

Learning Outcomes

By the end of this section you will:

- Have a better understanding of what the PEACE model of interviewing is and how it can be applied to achieve results.
- Have learnt some approaches to using effective questioning under the PEACE model, making use also of open and closed questions.
- Have some useful tips of how to best prepare for an interview using the PEACE model.
- Be aware of some things to consider when conducting an interview remotely rather than in person.
- Better understand the importance of the skills and different approaches to active listening to get the most from any interviewee.

- Know about some things to actively avoid when using active listening skills during an interview.
- Develop your appreciation of communication skills.

The PEACE Model

Following a series of false confessions in high-profile, serious criminal cases in the 1970s and 1980s, many people raised serious concerns about whether the existing police interviewing framework was too confrontational and obscure, with a focus on human behaviour that was either unreliable or else misinterpreted. In response, the Government commissioned a comprehensive review of police interviews that revealed serious flaws in the means used to question individuals and secure confessions which then turned out to be unreliable when scrutinised by a court of law. According to Professor John Baldwin, who published a report on police interviews in 1992, "*The main weaknesses that were identified were a lack of preparation, a general ineptitude, poor technique, an assumption of guilt, unduly repetitive, persistent or laboured questioning, a failure to establish the relevant facts, and the exertion of too much pressure.*".

This report led to the creation of a new investigative interviewing framework known as the PEACE method. Developed by a team of law enforcement professionals and psychologists, including Professor Baldwin, PEACE has since been incorporated into UK policing and is now part of the basic level of instruction for all police officers in England and Wales, and has been for many years. This approach has also been adopted by the professional private investigation sector.

The PEACE approach is a non-accusatory investigative technique that prioritises information gathering over securing a confession. The acronym stands for:

- **P:** preparation and planning.
- **E:** engage and explain.
- **A:** account, clarification and challenge.
- **C:** closure.
- **E:** evaluation.

How Does PEACE Work?

According to the College of Policing the model aims, "*...to obtain accurate and reliable accounts from victims, witnesses or suspects about matters* *under police investigation."*. As we will discuss later, it is very often good practice for the professional private investigator to at least closely mirror police practice even when there is no strict legal requirement to do so. In the context of interviewing witnesses, the PEACE model is equally relevant for all of the reasons police officers use it.

The model is grounded in an evidence-led, scientific approach. Research in cognitive psychology suggests that placing a greater emphasis upon obtaining high-quality information from the witness, rather than using subterfuge or pressure to secure a confession, will yield much more successful results. To this end the style adopted by the investigator conducting the interview will be much more informal and conversational, seeking to build rapport as the interview progresses. Instead of firing a series of closed questions at the interviewee, based very loosely on the pre-set agenda of the interviewer, the flow of the interview will follow the conversation – still structured, but less rigid than previous approaches. When done well the interviewee will be doing most of the talking and the interviewer most of the listening.

The Approach to Questions

The PEACE method uses a so-called 'hourglass' style of questioning. Firstly, an interviewer asks open questions to stimulate the interviewee's memory and get the conversation flowing. They then follow with closed or targeted lines of enquiry, before concluding with more open questions. The justification for this order centres largely on increasing the reliability and accuracy of the information the interviewee provides. Initial open questions should give the interviewee space to 'tell, explain and describe' (TED) without restriction, interruption or direction. At this stage, the objective should be to give the interviewee time to search their memory and recall as much information as possible, without having any recollections 'contaminated' by the interviewer.

The information gleaned from open questioning informs the second stage. At this point, the interviewer may use targeted questions to clarify certain details, obtain specific facts or explore inconsistencies. Questions here are often referred to as the '5W+H' questions, otherwise known as: who, why, what, where, when and how.

Concluding with more open questions can lighten the atmosphere, particularly if an interviewee has had to explain inaccuracies or relive upsetting incidents. This may make an interviewee more amenable to supplying further information if required. In extremely simplistic terms (and to somewhat mix our metaphors) this whole approach is characterised by deep sea trawling for information first followed by panning the river for the golden nuggets and finishing with a final trawl! So the questions may look something like this:

- **Stage one, open questions.** For example, "Tell me what happened last Wednesday morning?".
- **Stage two, closed questions.** For example, "What colour was the person's coat?".
- **Stage three, open questions.** For example, "Is there anything else you can recall about what happened?".

Good Cop Versus Bad Cop

It depends on the situation. The PEACE method emphasises building rapport between the interviewer and the interviewee. While it's crucial for the interviewer to remain calm, professional and in control, the interviewee must also feel relaxed enough to provide information freely and as they recall it, without feeling pressured to agree to details or give facts that they believe the interviewer wants to hear.

Interviewers should also be empathetic and mindful of any questions that may cause distress. Often, the information required by the interviewer pertains to incidents that could be embarrassing, traumatic or even illegal. If an interviewee is in a heightened emotional state, they may become defensive, obstructive or less reliable. Therefore, interviewers should avoid pressing an issue or repeating questions in a manner that could exacerbate the negative emotions of their interviewee.

However, persistent questioning is not unreasonable. If an interviewer suspects that the interviewee is withholding crucial details, they can continue to explore that subject, provided that they do so in a calm and respectful manner.

The Investigative State of Mind

- **A:** assume nothing.
- **B:** believe nothing.
- **C:** challenge everything.

Preparing for a PEACE Interview

Good preparation is the foundation of the PEACE method and essential for its success. Without adequate preparation, an interviewer may enter the interview room with biases, preconceptions or misinterpretations that could hinder their judgment and make subsequent questioning less effective.

Before an interview, interviewers should gather all available evidence and materials, such as CCTV footage, email correspondence or witness accounts. Careful examination of this material allows interviewers to build a comprehensive picture of the event, distinguishing between factual information and conjecture, and highlighting any gaps. Additionally, understanding the interviewee is crucial for a tailored interview and increases the likelihood of building rapport. At this stage, interviewers may prepare a few questions based on their knowledge, but these should be open and flexible, allowing for deviation based on new information.

With adequate preparation, interviewers should clearly define their aims and objectives. These may include corroborating evidence or disproving narratives. However, it's important to note that securing a confession is not a primary objective under the PEACE method.

Remote Interviews

When conducting interviews remotely, the PEACE model requires additional considerations. While preparation, questioning and evidence-gathering remain largely the same, physical cues and a sense of control differ. Helping the interviewee feel calm is arguably easier as they may feel more comfortable in their own environment. However, there's also a risk of the interviewee becoming disengaged and distracted, as long video meetings can be challenging to maintain focus on.

The presence of other individuals in the interviewee's room can influence their behaviour or restrict the amount of information they're willing to share. For the interviewer, visual cues are more challenging to discern on video and can easily be overlooked. Consequently, establishing rapport between the two participants becomes more intricate in an online setting compared to in-person interactions. Therefore, further research and development are necessary to enhance this technique's compatibility with online communication through video conferencing.

Active Listening Skills

Active listening is a crucial technique in conducting effective witness interviews. It involves paying close attention to the witness's words, asking follow-up questions, and clarifying any unclear information. Avoid interrupting the witness or making assumptions about their statements. This fosters trust and encourages them to provide more detailed and accurate information.

When conducting witness interviews, open questions are essential. They allow the witness to provide detailed and specific information, while closed questions, which can only be answered with a yes or no, limit the amount of information they can offer. Open questions help to uncover important details that might not have been mentioned in previous statements or reports.

Leading questions should be strictly avoided during witness interviews. They can influence the witness's response and potentially undermine the reliability of their testimony. Leading questions suggest a particular answer or include information that may bias the witness's response. Instead, questions should be neutral and objective, allowing the witness to express their perspective freely without external influence.

At the end of the witness interview, it's crucial to summarise the information provided and confirm your understanding of what the witness has said. This helps to prevent misunderstandings or miscommunications and provides an opportunity for the witness to clarify any unclear information.

While the words a witness speaks hold significance, their non-verbal cues can also offer valuable insights. As an investigator, it's crucial to pay close attention to the witness's body language, tone of voice and facial expressions. These cues can reveal clues about the witness's level of comfort, confidence and honesty. Additionally, it's essential to be mindful of your own non-verbal communication, as it can also influence the witness's responses.

Building Trust

Establishing trust with a witness is paramount for conducting an effective interview. Demonstrating respect, showing empathy and understanding, and upholding confidentiality are key factors in building trust. Avoid making unfulfilled promises or pressuring the witness to provide specific information. By building trust, the witness may be more inclined to provide accurate and detailed information.

Adapting to the Witness's Communication Style

This approach is also known as 'mirroring'. Each witness is unique and their communication preferences vary. As an investigator, it's vital to adapt your communication style to suit the witness's needs. Some witnesses may prefer a conversational approach, while others may prefer a more formal interview setting.

By adapting to the witness's communication style, you can create a more comfortable and conducive environment for the interview. As well as adjusting your tone to match the person you are speaking to you can also 'mirror' what they say, for example, repeating the last part of their previous sentence in a questioning style as though seeking confirmation. This then encourages them to continue speaking, perhaps adding extra detail. A word of caution, this must be used sparingly otherwise it can sound as though you are simply 'parroting' them and not listening properly so use only as appropriate!

Embrace the Silence

Silence can also be a powerful approach although can become awkward if overused and used for too long a period. The instinctive tendency for any of us in a conversation or interview is to fill a silence. In an interview this approach can encourage an interviewee to continue speaking when they have stopped. Silence is awkward and if it is clear from your own body language that you are not about to fill the void the interviewee will usually take the non-verbal cue and continue, either elaborating or otherwise expanding on the information they are providing you with. Like any of these approaches, this must not be overused as it will become obvious to the interviewee.

Recording the Interview

After conducting a witness interview, it's crucial to document the gathered information. This can be done through a written statement or a recording of the interview. Accurate documentation of the witness's responses is essential because this information might be presented as evidence in court. Additionally, it's important to keep the information confidential and ensure its secure storage.

In conclusion, effective witness interviews are a key component of any investigation. Thorough preparation, establishing rapport, active listening, using open questions, avoiding leading questions, summarising, confirming information, paying attention to non-verbal cues, building trust, adapting to the witness's communication style and documenting the interview are all essential techniques. These techniques, while requiring practice and skill, can be honed through experience and training. By employing these strategies, investigators can gather accurate and reliable information that helps to solve cases and/or present evidence in court.

MORE PIES

Building on the areas already discussed under Active Listening, this excellent mnemonic was developed by the FBI to assist crisis negotiators in remembering the crucial steps involved in active listening, especially when they're under pressure. This model could be useful in various situations:

Minimal encouragers. Use verbal and non-verbal communication, such as nodding, to show that you're listening and interested in what the person is saying.

Open-ended questions. Ask open questions instead of closed ones to encourage the person to provide more information.

Reflection. Repeat or echo recent words or phrases the person has used to demonstrate your understanding.

Effective pauses. Use silences before or after something meaningful to:

- Demonstrate understanding of the significance of the statement.
- Allow venting by providing a space for the person to express their frustration.
- Give time to think by allowing yourself time to process the information.
- Encourage turn-taking to promote a collaborative conversation.
- Help everyone focus by assisting everyone in concentrating on the discussion.

Paraphrase. Summarise what the person has been saying to demonstrate understanding.

'I' messages. Begin sentences with 'I' to personalise your statements, show responsibility and establish rapport.

Emotional labelling. Acknowledge and validate the person's emotions, for example, "I can see you're upset, this must be frustrating for you.".

Summary. Provide a concise summary of the conversation in your own words.

Refresher Check

What does PEACE stand for?

What is meant by the 'hourglass' style of questioning? Can you describe the three stages of the hourglass?

A useful way to remember to use open questions is the acronym TED. What does TED stand for?

What does the ABC of 'The Investigative State of Mind' refer to?

What are some of the things for the interviewer to consider when conducting a remote interview?

List three of the approaches to active listening that will assist the interviewer in getting the most from the interviewee and three things to avoid!

A useful way to remember to use active listening skills is with the mnemonic MORE PIES. What does this stand for?

Recommended Further Reading

'*Effective Interview Techniques: how to get the information you need*', Gateley Legal (January 2023)

'*The Science of Interviewing, PEACE: A Different Approach to Investigative Interviewing*', Forensic Investigative Solutions, Jonathan Davison (1992)

'*Investigative Interviewing: Psychology and Practice*', Rebecca Milne, Ray Bull (1999)

'*Investigative Interviewing: The Conversation Management Approach*', Eric Shepherd, Andy Griffiths (2013)

'*NPIA: National Investigative Interviewing Strategy*', National Policing Improvement Agency (2009)

'*Achieving Best Evidence in Criminal Proceedings: Guidance on interviewing victims and witnesses, and guidance on using special measures*', Ministry of Justice (2011)

'*Investigative Interviewing*', Ray Bull (1999)

'*Investigative Interviewing*', Authorised Professional Practice, College of Policing (2022)

'*Transform Your Investigative Interviews with the 5 Step PEACE Model*', Polonius Systems, Muznah Naeem (September 2022)

'*Memory-enhancing Techniques for Investigative Interviewing: the cognitive interview*', Fisher, R.P. & Geiselman, R.E. (1992)

'*Conflict Management Skills*', Authorised Professional Practice, College of Policing (2020)

Chapter Seven
Witness Statements

Introduction

The taking of a professional witness statement must be viewed as a core skill for any private investigator. In civil proceedings, as well as criminal proceedings, the witness statement forms the basis of the case. The contents, or omissions of any statements, will inevitably be the decisive factor in determining the strength, or weakness, of any case before it is heard in court. It is vital therefore that the professional private investigator is aware of the necessary 'points to prove' and, where the witness is able to honestly attest to any such points, that these are properly covered in their witness statement.

Note also that it is the witnesses' statement and not the statement of the person taking it. The skilled statement taker will be able to obtain a statement that reads like the statement of that person, in language that they would use and giving evidence to facts that are known to them and not the person taking it.

Learning Outcomes

By the end of this section you will:

- Be aware of some common terms used in civil proceedings where evidence is concerned.
- Be familiar with Section 32 of the Civil Procedure Rules covering evidence.
- Know what is meant by Statements of Case.
- Understand what a witness statement is, how it is prepared and then compiled.
- Know the importance of drafting a statement as well as the Statement of Truth.
- Have learnt about the importance of not making false statements.
- Have learnt about considerations around the instruction of expert witnesses when advising clients during case management discussions.

- Have a better understanding of the importance of disclosure and exchange of witness statements as well as some important things to consider before exchange.
- Understand what can and cannot be done in terms of telephone statements and electronic signatures.

Evidence of Witnesses – General Rule

Section 32 of the Civil Procedure Rules covers evidence for civil proceedings in the UK. The general rule is that any fact that has to be proved by the evidence of witnesses, is to be proved at trial by their oral evidence given in public and/or at any other hearing, by their evidence in writing. This is subject to any provision to the contrary contained in these Rules or elsewhere, or to any order of the court. The court may give directions:

- Identifying or limiting the issues to which factual evidence may be directed.
- Identifying the witnesses who may be called or whose evidence may be read.
- Limiting the length or format of witness statements.

Statements of Case: Impact on Evidential Issues

When starting a claim, a claimant must set out what it believes to be the relevant facts of the dispute in a document known as the Particulars of Claim. This will be served on the defendant at the same time as, or very shortly after, the claim form. A defendant who wishes to dispute the claim must then serve a defence. Together the Particulars of Claim and defence are known as the Statements of Case. A defendant has three ways to respond to the matters set out in the Particulars of Claim:

1. A defendant may choose to admit certain facts. Once something is admitted it is deemed to be accepted as fact, so an admission should only be made in respect of uncontested facts. It is not normally open for a party to withdraw an admission once made.
2. A defendant may choose to deny certain facts. This means that those facts are in dispute and both sides will have to present evidence at trial to set out their cases in relation to those facts.

3. A defendant may 'not admit' certain facts. This does not necessarily mean that the defendant disputes those matters, but requires the claimant to prove them.

Once the Particulars and defence have been exchanged the parties will understand what issues are in dispute and need to be proved, and which facts are now common ground.

Glossary of Common Terms

Disclosure. The process of showing the relevant evidence to the other party.

Expert evidence. This is evidence of an expert's opinion, of what they think or believe about something.

'Hot-tubbing'. This is when you have two or more expert witnesses and they give their evidence at the same time instead of, or as well as, being cross examined individually. This is also known as Concurrent Expert Evidence (CEE).

Liability. Proving that the problem is legally the defendant's fault – they breached your legal rights or broke a contract with you.

Quantum. The amount of compensation your claim is worth.

Simultaneous exchange. This is when the parties to a case exchange their witness statements at the same time on the same day.

Statement of Truth. The last and standalone paragraph at the end of a witness statement declaring that the facts stated in the statement are true. There is also a Statement of Truth at the end of a claim form or Particulars of Claim or Schedule of Loss, declaring that the contents are true.

Witness statement. A document in which someone explains what they saw, did or heard.

What is a Witness Statement?

A witness statement is a formal written document utilised in English and Welsh courts during litigation. It comprises an individual's candid account of facts pertinent to a dispute, based on their personal knowledge.

The primary purpose of a witness statement is to inform the parties and the court of evidence a party intends to rely upon during trial to bolster their case. It will be considered by the judge, in conjunction with all other evidence, to form a judgment based on the most probable occurrence. Witness statements are not intended to present arguments or case documents.

How Will it Be Prepared?

There are typically three stages in the preparation of a witness statement:

1. **Initial scoping discussion.** Typically, lawyers acting for the party which has asked the witness to give evidence will get in touch with the witness to discuss the issues on which they are able to provide factual evidence.

2. **Fact-finding.** Once the scope of the witness statement has been initially determined, the lawyers will either meet or hold a call with the witness to obtain their recollection of the relevant facts. It is crucial for witnesses to distinguish between facts that they are personally aware of, having been directly involved or witnessing the event, and facts that they have been made aware of through other means. Inappropriate inclusion of the latter category in a witness statement may necessitate an explanation of how the witness obtained this information.

   If appropriate, the lawyers may request the witness to review certain documents related to the dispute or specific issues. A meticulous record of any documents reviewed will be necessary. Depending on the complexity of the dispute, the initial fact-finding exercise may be relatively brief. In some instances, it could be an extended process spanning several days. It may be necessary to reconvene for additional meeting or meetings.

3. **Draft witness statement.** Following the fact-finding discussions, the lawyers will often provide the witness with a first draft of a statement, based on their notes of the witness's evidence taken during those discussions. The first draft will often contain several queries for the witness to consider.

The statement must be the witness's account of the facts in their own words. Therefore, if anything in a draft statement is inaccurate, the witness must change it. If there are any words or phrases in a draft that the witness would not use, they should remove or reword the statement to reflect how they would describe the relevant scenario or recollection.

The statement may attach some relevant documents as an exhibit.

Statement of Truth

Upon completing their statement, the witness will be required to sign a Statement of Truth. This is a concluding statement at the end of a witness's statement, affirming the witness's belief in the veracity and accuracy of the facts presented. There is also a Statement of Truth at the end of a claim form or Particulars of Claim or schedule of loss declaring that the contents are true.

The standard wording of a Statement of Truth is, *"I affirm that the facts stated in this witness statement are true. I understand that proceedings for contempt of court may be initiated against any individual who makes or causes to be made a false statement in a document verified by a statement of truth without an honest belief in its truthfulness."*.

In cases involving business and property courts, and where the statement is intended for use at trial, witnesses are obligated to provide a confirmation, in a prescribed format, acknowledging their comprehension of the purpose of witness statements and their proper preparation.

In the [Court name] County Court   Case number

....

Parties	[Name]	Claimant
	[Name]	Defendant

WITNESS STATEMENT

1. I, [Name] of [Address] am [the Claimant in this claim]. The facts in this statement come from my personal knowledge [*or as the case may be*].
2. ....
3. ....
4. etc
5. I believe that the facts stated in this witness statement are true.

Signed

Dated

Witnesses may be subjected to cross-examination in court regarding the content of their witness statement. As the statement of truth explicitly acknowledges, proceedings for contempt of court may also be brought against an individual who makes a false statement in a document signed by a statement of truth without an honest belief in its truthfulness. Therefore, it is paramount that witnesses possess a comprehensive understanding of the content of their witness statement.

False Statements: UK Civil Procedure Rules 32.14

Proceedings for contempt of court may be initiated against an individual who fabricates or causes a false statement to be included in a document prepared in anticipation of or during proceedings, and subsequently verified by a statement of truth without a genuine belief in its veracity.

Who Will Get to See the Witness Statement?

After a witness signs their statement, a copy of it, along with any other witness statements, will be provided to the opposing party. In cases where witness statements are required for trial, the opposing party will usually provide them simultaneously.

After the exchange of witness statements, a witness may have the opportunity to review the opposing party's witness statements that address the issues raised in their own evidence. Sometimes, it may be necessary to prepare a supplemental witness statement, for instance, when corrections or clarifications are required in response to the opposing party's witness statements.

If the matter proceeds to trial, once a witness has given their evidence in court based on their statement, it will usually be available to non-parties, such as the press, during the trial. After the trial, such non-parties would need to request court permission to access the statement.

Expert Witness Statements

These witnesses are individuals who provide expert opinions in legal proceedings. Their evidence, known as expert evidence, is presented in a written document called an expert's report. This report delves into the expert's thoughts and beliefs on a subject they are considered experts in.

A judge will only consider an expert's opinion if it is relevant to the dispute. For instance, a doctor's opinion on the likelihood of full recovery from an accident would be relevant in a medical malpractice case.

Expert witness reports are not typically included in small claims cases unless the court specifically permits it (except in cases of personal injury).

In fast-track claims, expert witness reports are commonly used, but their contents may not be in dispute. In such cases, the expert's testimony may not be necessary in court, and their attendance could significantly increase the costs of the case. Additionally, their availability may limit the trial timeline.

When Should I Seek Expert Evidence?

Consider carefully before relying on expert evidence. It's an expensive step and even though you're paying the expert's fees, their primary purpose is to assist the court not you. This means that they may express opinions you disagree with, and you have no control over that. However, there are cases where expert evidence can be crucial in supporting certain aspects of your case. For instance, in a personal injury case, a medical report from an appropriate medical expert is essential. To ensure impartiality, it's usually best to choose an expert who hasn't been involved in your case in any way. You should typically select someone who isn't treating you directly. Expert's reports, particularly those from medical experts, can be time-consuming to obtain and costly.

An expert witness must maintain independence. Their duty to the court surpasses their duty to you. Even if you requested their opinion and paid their fees, they may provide information that contradicts your case. While the expert's report may be considered 'your' evidence, any party can use it as evidence during the trial. Carefully consider whether to ask the expert any questions and, if so, what questions to ask and how to present them. Be prepared for potential unfavourable responses.

Documentary Evidence: Disclosure

Disclosure of documents is often a crucial part of a civil dispute. It typically occurs early in the claim, after the exchange of Statements of Case. The parties are obligated to disclose all relevant documents in their possession or control, not just those that support their case. This duty of disclosure persists throughout the case, meaning that additional documents that may emerge later must also be disclosed. If a party believes that the other side has failed to disclose all necessary documents, they can apply to the court for an order requiring them to do so.

The evidence that must be produced during disclosure includes electronic documents, such as emails and electronic files stored on computers and other media like mobile devices. Each party is required to sign a disclosure statement to the court confirming their compliance with their duties of disclosure.

Disclosure is a pivotal stage in any court proceedings as it is usually the first time each party sees the full extent of the other party's documents. Consequently, many cases settle shortly after disclosure is completed. The rules governing disclosure are intricate and can be found in Part 31 of the Civil Procedure Rules.

Exchange of Witness Statements

The order for directions in your case (the list of steps the court sends to each side, explaining what must be done and by when) will indicate when you and the other side must exchange your witness statements.

Typically, the court orders the sides to exchange witness statements after disclosure. This is standard practice because otherwise you wouldn't benefit from the information you gain from the other side's documents. For instance, you might discover something that supports your case and want to bring it to the court's attention. You can do this by mentioning it in your statement. Alternatively, you might find something that threatens your case. You have the opportunity to explain the circumstances or offer a different explanation in your statement. If you have a witness but decide not to use their evidence, there's no need to provide their statement to the other party.

Witness statements must be exchanged simultaneously. This means both sides exchange statements on the same day. Simultaneous exchange is intended to prevent one side or witness from seeing the other side's statements before writing their own and possibly gaining an advantage from seeing what the other side's witnesses say before you write yours. You can only be certain that simultaneous exchange occurs if you agree to exchange statements in person. However, this is rarely done due to inconvenience. Instead, you all agree to exchange statements via email on a specific day and time or by posting them on the same day. If you post them, obtain a certificate of posting from the post office in case of any disputes later.

Before sending your statement, double-check that the other party is also sending theirs simultaneously. Contact them or their advisor to confirm that they're ready to exchange. For instance, you could say, "Do you agree that we'll email our statements to each other immediately after this call ends?". Agree that neither party should open the other's witness statements until you both confirm receipt. Common email-related issues include attachment size exceeding limits, spam filtering, or incorrect email addresses causing delivery failures. Maintain a written record of all exchange-related conversations. Note down key points discussed, the date and time of the conversation and any relevant details.

If the other party fails to prepare their witness statements in time to exchange them before the deadline specified in the order for directions, consider using informal pressure, such as phoning or emailing them to request immediate preparation. Clearly state that if they don't comply, you'll have to return to court. Specify the date and time of this action. If you contact them via phone, follow-up with a letter. If this approach doesn't yield results, you may need to seek court intervention. Apply for an order requiring the other party to exchange witness statements within a specified timeframe, for example, seven days. If they fail to comply, the court may strike out their claim, defence or counterclaim. Be prepared to pay a fee and request that the defendant reimburse you for this expense.

Caution! If you exchange witness statements by sending them attached to an email, it is far better to send them as pdf documents or as scans. If you send them as Word attachments, there is software that allows the other side to read the changes you have made in the course of preparing your statements.

Telephone Statements and Electronic Signatures

There's no legal requirement for a witness statement to be signed in ink on paper (a 'wet signature') or that a document be signed in a specific manner. The common law in England and Wales has always been flexible in recognising various types of signatures. The courts have accepted electronic forms of signatures, such as a name typed at the bottom of an email or clicking an 'I accept' tick box on a website. Signatures can be captured in different ways when associated with digital documents:

- As a graphical digital representation of the witness's usual signature (typed version).
- As a scanned copy of a 'wet signature' (if the witness has the facilities to do so).
- Using a digital signature authorised or certified by the maker.
- Using a password (an email from a named email account could also be considered to 'purport to be signed' by the account holder, especially if it's a secure account and requires a password to access).

All these methods appear to purport to be signatures for the purposes of both the Criminal Justice Act 1967 and the Magistrates' Courts Act 1980.

The Electronic Communications Act 2000 (ECA 2000) specifically states that the use of digital signatures is admissible as evidence in any legal proceedings. Section 7 of ECA 2000 states that an electronic signature incorporated into or logically associated with a particular electronic communication or data, along with the certification by any person of such a signature, will be admissible in any legal proceedings to establish the authenticity or integrity of any communication or data.

Refresher Check

Section 32 of the Civil Procedure Rules covers evidential matters. Under the General Rule there are three areas in which the court may give direction. Can you list them?

When starting a claim, a claimant must set out what it believes to be the relevant facts of the dispute in a document. What is this known as?

What are the three ways in which a defendant can respond to the matters set out in the Particulars of Claim?

What is the primary purpose of a witness statement?

There are typically three stages in the preparation of a witness statement. Can you list them?

With regard to the Statement of Truth, which of the following statements is correct?:
- A verbal statement made by a witness prior to providing a written statement.
- A signed declaration made at the beginning of any written statement affirming the witness's belief in the veracity and accuracy of the facts presented.
- A signed declaration made at the end of any written statement affirming the witness's belief in the veracity and accuracy of the facts presented.

If matters proceed to a trial, at what point would a non-party be able to get access to any written witness statement?

An expert witness can only lawfully provide testimony in support of the case of the person who instructed them. True or false?

What are three forms of signature acceptable to civil courts as proof of signature?

Recommended Further Reading

'Witness Statements in England and Wales', Pinsent Masons (June 2024)

'Witness Statements and Expert Reports', Advicenow (March 2024)

'Evidence in Civil Disputes', IBB Law (2022)

Guidance on UK Civil Procedure Rules at www.justice.gov.uk

Guidance on Victims and Witnesses, Crown Prosecution Service at www.cps.gov.uk

Chapter Eight
Open Source Intelligence

Introduction

Imagine you are trying to find an old friend you've lost touch with, or perhaps you are curious about a company advertising a job that seems too good to be true. Where do you start? The answer lies in something called Open Source Intelligence (OSINT). OSINT is all about gathering useful information from publicly available sources – social media, websites, news articles or even a photo someone posted online. It's not hacking or spying, it's simply making sense of what's already out there and publicly available.

For beginners, OSINT might sound like something only detectives or tech wizards use but it's more accessible than you think. Whether you are a student, a journalist or just someone who loves a good puzzle, learning the basics can open doors to understanding the world in new ways. This chapter will walk you through some simple techniques to get started. We will cover how to dig into people, places and online spaces without needing advanced tools – just curiosity and a bit of patience. Plus, we will explore a real-world example to see these skills in action and tackle an important topic for anyone in the UK, that is, how privacy laws like GDPR affect what we do. By the end, you will have a solid foundation to build on, whether you are writing a report or satisfying your own curiosity.

Learning Outcomes

By the end of this section you will:

- Have a better understanding of the legal framework as well as the difference between information and intelligence.
- Learn about different categories of OSINT, including social media, public records and databases, online forums and communities as well as others and some of the most common techniques for exploiting them.
- Understand the importance of so-called 'sock puppet' accounts, why they are effective and how, as well as some of the legal and ethical considerations to consider when using them.

Core OSINT Techniques

Let's dive into the nuts and bolts of OSINT. Here are five key areas to get you started, each with enough detail to give you a good foundation upon which to build.

1: People Search Basics

Finding someone online starts with what you already know – a name, a job, maybe a city. The trick is to use search engines cleverly. Start with Google. Type the name in quotes, for example, "John Smith", to narrow it down. Add a location or keyword like "London" or "teacher" to filter out the dozens of John Smiths who aren't your guy. It is also worth checking public records too, such as the UK's Electoral Roll (available via some council websites or services like 192.com), but don't expect miracles – people can opt out. Beyond Google, try Bing or DuckDuckGo, they sometimes return different results. There is always a chance that other search engines might return something that Google missed.

Other useful sources are the various professional directories, for example, Companies House for business owners or professional bodies like the Law Society for solicitors. If, for example, you are trying to build up an intelligence picture on a "Dr Sarah Brown" in Leeds a quick check on the General Medical Council's register could confirm she is legitimate. Don't stop at one source, cross-check everything. If Sarah is listed as a GP but a local forum calls her a vet, dig deeper. Patience is key, you might sift through twenty irrelevant hits before striking gold. If you hit a wall, tweak your terms. Swap "Sarah Brown" for "S Brown" or add a middle initial from a stray LinkedIn profile. It's like panning for nuggets of gold in a stream – slow, steady and rewarding when it works.

2: Social Media Investigations

Social media is an OSINT goldmine. Platforms like X, LinkedIn and Instagram are packed with clues. Start with a username search. Many people reuse the same handle across sites. Tools like Namechk.com can help you see where a username pops up. Once you are on a profile, look at posts, followers and tagged photos. On X, for instance, someone's posts might reveal their daily routine or opinions. Just remember, what's public today might vanish tomorrow, so screenshot anything useful.

Let's consider how this might work in a real-world scenario. For example, @LondonBaker. You find their Twitter moaning about early Tube delays – likely a Londoner. Their Instagram's got cake pics tagged #BakingClass and a follower list includes @SohoCookSchool. A quick hop to LinkedIn might show a baker in Soho matching the name. This crisscross approach with each platform adds a piece to the puzzle. It's similar to hopping across a series of stepping stones in a fast flowing river to get to the other side. Watch for privacy settings though. If they have gone private you are stuck with what's already out there. Hashtags are another trick. Search #LondonEvents on Instagram and you might spot @LondonBaker at a fair. Even comments matter. Someone replying, "Great to meet you at the market!" pins them to a place and time. It's less about tech and more about noticing the little things, like a detective reading between the lines of a chatty suspect.

3: Website and Domain Analysis

Ever wonder who is behind a website? Tools such as WHOIS lookups (try whois.domaintools.com) to see who registered a domain, including their name or email (unless they have hidden it with privacy settings). You can also use archive.org's Wayback Machine to peek at old versions of a site. Say a company claims to have been around for decades but their site only goes back two years – that's a red flag.

Let's consider this in the scenario of a so-called 'vintage watch dealer' at oldtimewatches.co.uk. A WHOIS check shows it was registered six months ago to a generic privacy-protected email. Suspicious? Dig into the Wayback Machine – nothing before last year. Compare that to a legitimate site registered in 2005 with a real name attached. It is always worth digging deeper into the site content too – right click and 'view source' to spot sloppy code or copied text. Link it with socials. If their Twitter's @OldTimeWatches but only started tweeting last month, it's a pattern. Even dead links or outdated 'Contact Us' pages can hint at neglect or a scam. It's about building a picture. A site's history, ownership and consistency scream louder than its glossy homepage ever could.

4: Imagery and Geolocation

Photos can tell stories that words can't and Google Reverse Image Search is an invaluable tool in this regard. Upload a picture and it will show you where else it has appeared online. For geolocation, look for landmarks or street signs in the background. Tools like Google Earth can help you match a blurry hill or building to a real place. It's like being a digital Sherlock Holmes, piecing together clues from a single snap that may have been taken to tell one story but actually tells another in the background.

For example, if you have a photo of a friend at a 'secret spot' – a cliff, some waves, no caption. Reverse Image Search it. Maybe it's popped up on a

Cornwall tourism blog. No luck? Zoom in, a faded sign says Porth. Google "Porth beaches Cornwall", and Porthtowan fits the cliff shape. Open Google Earth, drag the little yellow pegman into Street View and there's your cliff. Details matter. Cloud patterns, shadows, even litter can date or place it. A well-defined shadow at noon might mean summer; a Coke can design could narrow it to post-2020. It's slow work, but once you match that pixelated blob to a real spot, it's pure magic. Practise on your own pictures first. Find your local park in a selfie and you are halfway there.

5: Simple Tools for OSINT

You don't need to be a wealthy tech genius. Freebies like Maltego (for linking data) or X Pro (formerly known as TweetDeck for monitoring X in real-time) on a paid subscription are useful tools. Even your browser's incognito mode is handy as it keeps your searches from getting muddled by your own history. Start small, experiment and you'll be surprised by what you uncover.

Another useful tool is Hunchly. It's a browser add-on that tracks every site you visit in a case, perfect for keeping tabs without losing your place. Or grab OSINT Framework (osintframework.com), a clickable tree of free tools – think phone number lookups or email verifiers.

Some experienced OSINT operators make good use of Google Dorks too. Type "site:*.edu filetype:pdf 'John Smith'" to find academic papers by a John Smith. It's geeky but simple once you get the hang of it. Even Excel can be your friend. Dump usernames into a spreadsheet, sort and spot patterns. The trick? Don't drown in options. Pick one tool, such as X Pro, and track a hashtag for a day. See what clicks. It's less about the kit and more about how you wield it.

These techniques are your toolkit. They're straightforward, but they take practise. You will see them in action with a case study towards the end of this chapter.

'Sock Puppets': An Overview

So-called 'sock puppet' accounts are fictitious online identities created to deceive or manipulate digital communities. The term draws from the whimsical image of a sock transformed into a puppet, controlled covertly by a hand. In the digital realm, these puppets are managed by individuals or groups aiming to mask their true identity. Often, they serve to amplify agendas, evade restrictions or distort perceptions of consensus without revealing the puppeteer's role.

Common Uses and Motivations

These accounts are deployed in diverse contexts. In politics, they may masquerade as grassroots supporters to artificially inflate support for candidates or policies (a practice termed 'astroturfing'). On e-commerce platforms, sock puppets post fraudulent reviews to boost or sabotage products. In online forums, users banned for misconduct might resurrect access via new pseudonyms. Others exploit anonymity to harass opponents or shield their reputation while spreading controversial views. Motivations range from financial gain and ideological promotion to personal vendettas or simple trolling.

A professional private investigator in the UK could use sock puppet accounts as a tool to gather information secretly. For instance, where the investigator is hired to check if someone is cheating on their partner. They might create a fake social media profile. For example, 'Emma from Manchester, a thirty-something fitness fan', and use it online to follow the person they are investigating. By liking posts or joining local fitness groups the target is in, the investigator can watch their activity without raising suspicion. Another example could be where an investigator is looking into an insurance fraud case. They might set up a sock puppet as 'Dave, a car enthusiast' to chat in online forums about car accidents, hoping the target brags about faking a crash for a payout.

The benefits of this approach are pretty clear. Firstly, it keeps the the investigator's real identity hidden, which is crucial when needing to stay discreet. Nobody is going to open up if they know a private investigator is watching! Secondly, it lets them blend into online spaces, such as Facebook groups or X threads, where people share all sorts of personal information. For example, 'Emma' might spot the cheating partner posting flirty comments on a gym selfie, giving the investigator solid evidence. It's a cheap and flexible way to dig up information without needing expensive tools – just a laptop and some creativity.

But there are drawbacks too. For one, it's a legal grey area in the UK. Pretending to be someone else online isn't always illegal, but if the investigator uses the account to trick people into sharing private information or breaks platform rules (like Facebook's real-name policy), they could get into trouble – or even face a ban. Another downside is trust. If the target figures out that 'Dave' isn't real, for example, because the account is too new or the investigator slips up on car terminology, it could blow the whole investigation. Plus, it takes time to make a sock puppet believable, a blank profile with no history looks dodgy. So while sock puppets can be a sneaky advantage, they come with risks that the professional investigator has to weigh carefully.

GDPR and OSINT: What it is and Why it Matters

Now let's cover something critical for UK readers – the General Data Protection Regulation (GDPR). It's a law that governs how we handle personal data and it's a big deal when you're doing OSINT. Whether you're tracking a missing person or researching a company, you need to know the rules. OSINT uses public data, but public doesn't mean free-for-all.

A professional private investigator working in the UK must navigate a complex legal landscape when using OSINT as an investigative tool, particularly with the GDPR to be considered. GDPR, enacted to protect personal data and privacy, applies to any individual or organisation processing the personal data of UK or EU residents, regardless of where the processing occurs. For an investigator, OSINT (gathering publicly available information from sources like social media, news articles or public records) can be a goldmine. But it's also a potential minefield if not handled with care. A UK-based investigator can stay compliant while leveraging OSINT effectively by understanding what constitutes personal data under GDPR. This is critical. Names, addresses, phone numbers, IP addresses, social media profiles and even photos can fall under this umbrella. Even though OSINT relies on publicly available information, GDPR still applies if this data identifies an individual. An investigator must establish a lawful basis for processing this data. Typically, this could be 'legitimate interests' (Article 6(1)(f)), where the investigator's need to investigate balances against the individual's rights and freedoms. For example, investigating a fraud case might justify collecting data, but digging into someone's private life without cause wouldn't. The investigator should document this reasoning clearly as accountability is a cornerstone of GDPR.

Transparency is another key principle. While investigators often work discreetly, GDPR requires informing individuals about data collection unless an exemption applies. The 'detection and prevention of crime' exemption (under the UK Data Protection Act 2018, which complements GDPR) might allow an investigator to skip notification if informing the subject would prejudice an investigation, for example, tracking a suspect's public social media posts in a missing persons case. However, this exemption isn't a free pass – it must be proportionate and justified.

Data minimisation is equally important. An investigator should only collect what's necessary for the investigation. Scraping an entire social media profile when only a recent post is relevant could breach GDPR. Tools like web crawlers or OSINT platforms, for example, Maltego or SpiderFoot, can amplify efficiency, but they also risk over-collection. The investigator should filter and limit data at the source, ensuring they are not hoarding irrelevant details that could later be challenged.

Storage and security matter too. OSINT-derived data must be kept secure. Encrypted files, password-protected devices and restricted access are non-negotiable. GDPR mandates that data be retained only as long as necessary. If a case closes, the investigator should delete irrelevant personal data unless there is a legal obligation to keep it, like for billing or regulatory compliance. A retention policy, for example, 'delete after six months unless required', helps to demonstrate compliance.

Finally, working with clients adds another layer. If an investigator processes data on behalf of a client, for example, a law firm, they may become a 'data processor' under GDPR, requiring a contract outlining responsibilities. Even as an independent 'data controller', the investigator must ensure that their client's instructions align with GDPR. Investigating a cheating spouse at a client's whim might not hold up as a legitimate interest.

To tie it all together, a UK investigator should conduct regular GDPR training, maintain detailed records of data processing activities and consult the ICO guidance when in doubt. By balancing investigative needs with privacy rights, they can wield OSINT powerfully yet lawfully. Compliance isn't just about avoiding fines. It builds trust, which is priceless in the private investigation business.

Practical Tips for Staying Compliant

There are five golden rules:

1. **Purpose.** Only collect what you need. Sarah didn't dig into Tom's mates' lives, just his.
2. **Transparency.** If you are contacting people (like the car club), explain why you are asking.
3. **Storage.** Don't hoard data. Once Sarah found Tom she didn't need those screenshots.
4. **Consent.** If you are unsure, ask permission. Sharing Tom's photo publicly was a risk. Better to check with him first.
5. **Anonymity.** When possible, strip out personal details before sharing findings.

For beginners, GDPR might feel like a thrill ride, but it's also about respect. OSINT is powerful because it's public, not because it's sneaky. Stick to ethical lines. You'll stay legal and sleep better.

Information Versus Intelligence

As a professional investigator it is important to understand the difference between information and intelligence. In the use of OSINT it is particularly important. The distinction between 'information' and 'intelligence' is subtle yet significant, often hinging on purpose, processing and application. Both terms are frequently encountered in areas like national security, policing, education and even everyday decision-making, but they serve different roles.

Information refers to raw, unprocessed data or facts. It's the building blocks – discrete pieces of knowledge that exist without necessarily being interpreted or connected. For example, in the UK, the Met Office might collect data on rainfall levels across London: '12mm fell in Camden at 3pm'. That's information – factual, standalone and neutral. Similarly, a police officer might note a car's registration plate or a bystander's statement after an incident. It's useful but lacks depth until something is done with it. Information is everywhere in the UK's data-driven society, from NHS patient records to the Office for National Statistics on population growth. It's abundant, accessible and often public-facing, like the latest GDP figures or train timetables.

Intelligence, however, is what emerges when information is processed, analysed and given context or meaning. It's about turning those raw facts into something actionable or insightful. Take the rainfall data – if the Met Office combines it with historical trends, wind patterns and flood risk maps to predict a potential Thames overflow, that's intelligence: information transformed into a tool for decision-making. In a policing context, the National Crime Agency might gather disparate bits of information – phone records, travel logs, witness tips and piece them together to identify a trafficking network. That synthesis, that leap from 'what' to 'so what', is intelligence. It's less about the data itself and more about the story it tells or the advantage it provides. As the police use the information to intelligence process so must an effective and professional private investigator.

The UK's legal and institutional frameworks highlight this divide. The Freedom of Information Act 2000, for instance, gives citizens access to raw data held by public bodies – minutes of council meetings or hospital spending figures. But intelligence, particularly in security contexts, is guarded tightly. Agencies like MI5 or Government Communications Headquarters (GCHQ) don't just collect phone calls or emails (information). They analyse patterns, assess threats and produce intelligence to thwart terrorism. The Investigatory Powers Act 2016 governs how such information is gathered and turned into intelligence, balancing security needs with privacy concerns, a debate that's raged in the UK for years.

Culturally, too, the distinction resonates. UK citizens might pride themselves on a 'well-informed' public, with various news outlets delivering facts nightly. Yet intelligence, whether it's a shrewd political strategy or a farmer's knack for reading weather beyond the forecast, carries a sense of mastery or cunning. In education, the shift from rote learning (information) to critical thinking (intelligence) reflects this value.

Ultimately, information is the 'what', while intelligence is the 'why' or 'how'. In the UK, where data flows freely but actionable insight drives everything from counter-terrorism to economic policy, the difference isn't just academic, it's practical. Information tells you that the Tube is delayed, intelligence tells you why and how to avoid it next time. One is a fact, the other is a superpower.

Conclusion

OSINT is like a treasure hunt. With a few simple tools and a curious mind, you can uncover amazing things. We've explored how to search for people, navigate social media, analyse websites and even pinpoint a photo's location. All of these can be learnt about in much more detail in any one of several good publications available on the market. The following case study shows how these skills solved real problems, while GDPR reminded us to keep our inquisitiveness in check and legal.

OSINT is a versatile and powerful tool for private investigators in the UK. By leveraging publicly available information and combining it with advanced analytical techniques, investigators can uncover critical insights while staying within legal and ethical boundaries. As technology evolves, so too must the skills and tools of the modern investigator, ensuring that OSINT remains a cornerstone of effective investigative work. This chapter provides a foundation for investigators to integrate OSINT into their practice, empowering them to conduct thorough and professional investigations. You are just starting, so don't worry about mastering it all overnight. Pick one technique, for example, a Google search tweak and try it out. The more you practise, the sharper you'll get. OSINT isn't just for professionals, it's for anyone who wants to understand the world a bit better. Keep exploring, stay ethical and who knows what you will discover next?

OSINT Training Exercise

Case Study: Tracking a Missing Person

Meet Sarah, a worried sister in Bristol. Her brother Tom, 28, hasn't been heard from in two weeks. He's a mechanic who loves cars and posts about them online. Sarah knows his full name (Tom Evans), his last job at a garage in Cardiff and his Instagram handle, @TomTheWrench. She's got a photo he posted last month, a blurry shot of him by a river with a bridge in the background. Can OSINT help her find him?

Step 1: People Search

Sarah starts with Google: "Tom Evans" + "Cardiff" + "mechanic". Too many hits. She refines it to "Tom Evans Cardiff garage" and finds a local news article about a car show where a Tom Evans from Ace Repairs won a prize six months ago. A quick search confirms Ace Repairs exists. Maybe he still works there.

Step 2: Social Media Dive

On Instagram, @TomTheWrench hasn't posted in three weeks, but his bio says, "Fixing rides & chasing rivers." His last post is the river photo. Sarah checks his followers – roughly fifty people, including @CardiffGearHeads, a car club. She finds their X account and sees Tom tagged in a post from three weeks ago at a meet-up. No recent activity, though.

Step 3: Website Check

The car club's site (cardiffgearheads.co.uk) lists past events. A WHOIS lookup shows it is registered to a local enthusiast. The Wayback Machine reveals Tom's name on a 2024 roster, confirming he's active in the scene. Sarah emails the club's contact, asking if they have seen him.

Step 4: Geolocation

That river photo is the key. Sarah uploads it to Google Reverse Image Search but there are no matches. She studies it – a stone bridge, a wide river, some trees. Could it be the River Taff in Cardiff? She opens Google Earth, zooms to the Taff and spots a bridge that looks close – Pont-y-Werin. The angle is off, but it's a start. She posts the photo to a local Cardiff Facebook group, asking if anyone recognises it. A reply points her to a spot near Llandaff.

Step 5: Pulling It Together

A club member replies. Tom was at the last meet-up but mentioned heading to a mate's cabin near Llandaff to 'get off-grid'. Sarah calls the garage. Tom quit a month ago. With the geolocation lead, she contacts local police who check the area and find Tom – safe but without his phone after a hiking mishap.

Lessons Learned

This case shows OSINT's power. Basic searches, social media and a photo led Sarah to Tom. For beginners, it's about starting with what you know, cross-checking, and being persistent. Tools helped, but common sense sealed the deal.

Refresher Check

Can you list three of the key areas of OSINT and give an example of each?

Public records and databases are a valuable source of information. Can you identify three locations where you might be able to access public records?

'Sock-puppet' accounts are used in a variety of ways. Can you list three of them?

If information is available to the public, it means it is free to be used however the investigator sees fit. Is this true or false?

Under GDPR, various categories of information fall within the definition of 'personal data'. Can you list three?

There are five golden rules listed for staying compliant with GDPR. Can you list them with a short descriptor of each?

Can you describe, in simple terms, the difference between information and intelligence?

Recommended Further Reading

'The OSINT Handbook: a practical guide to gathering and analysing online information', First Edition, Dale Meredith (March 2024)

'OSINT Techniques: Resources for Uncovering Online Information', Eleventh Edition, Michael Bazzell and Jason Edison (November 2024)

'Open Source Intelligence Methods and Tools', First Edition, Nihad A. Hassan and Rami Hijazi (July 2018)

'Offensive Intelligence: 300 techniques, tools and tips to know everything about everyone, in companies and elsewhere', Philippe Dylewski (June 2023)

Chapter Nine
Cyber Security

Introduction

In the previous chapter we looked at OSINT and how effective it can be in supporting investigations. The reason it is successful however is precisely because, as the name suggests, the source material is open – often when it shouldn't be! For the professional private investigator, cyber security should be viewed as the other side of the same coin. In order to not only properly advise clients but also to protect their own confidential records, particularly as a small business, professional investigators should have a sound working knowledge of current cyber security measures as well as putting those principles into practise in the running of their own business.

Modern technology is all around us – in the home, the workplace and the wider environment in which we all live and work every day. It's become a fundamental part of modern life. The internet has brought the world within easy reach. We all depend on it whether we realise it or not and whether we want to or not, at home and at work.

Data is now one of the most valuable commodities in the world. Particularly personal data, which describes our spending habits, our movements and our preferences across a broad spectrum of everyday life – our political choices, our browsing history and anything involving the press of a key. This means that our data is a prime target for cyber crime. Online criminals and hackers want to get their hands on our data and it can be easy to be taken in by their criminal techniques without ever being aware that we are the target of criminal activity. It's important to know what to look out for and what steps to take if subterfuge succeeds. That's where cyber security comes in.

The primary function of any cyber security measure is to protect the devices we use and the data we store on them from theft, damage and unauthorised access. It may seem daunting, but cyber security is driven by people, not technology, so we can all do our bit. People are responsible for what happens to their data and we all have far more control than we might realise. Much of the work to protect us is done behind the scenes, either by our employers or by the providers of goods and services. Despite that, however, we can also all play an important part in protecting ourselves.

Learning Outcomes

By the end of this section you will:
- Understand what phishing looks like and how to protect against it.
- Have learnt about the importance of using strong passwords.
- Understand how to keep your devices secure and up-to-date.
- Have learnt how to protect your devices from unauthorised access on the go, in the office and at home.
- Understand the dangers of unprotected Wi-Fi.
- Have learnt how to browse the web safely.
- Understand the dangers of third-party apps and warnings.

Why Cyber Security Matters

An increasing number of organisations are being seriously impacted by cyber incidents, for example, a phishing attempt to steal money and passwords or a ransomware attack that encrypts files preventing access. Why is this happening? There can be several reasons:

- Many cyber incidents are not targeted. They can affect any organisation that doesn't employ basic levels of protection.
- Organisations hold sensitive information. For example, organisation records, employee data, customer payment information, passwords and commercially sensitive information. All of this must be kept safe and confidential.
- Cyber criminals want to make money. They understand that an organisation's information is often of sufficient importance to that organisation that they would be prepared to pay a ransom to get it back.

Who is Behind Cyber Attacks?

- Online criminals are very good at identifying what can be monetised. For example, stealing and selling sensitive data or holding systems and information to ransom.
- Hackers have varying levels of expertise, often acting in an untargeted way to test their own skills or to cause disruption for the sake of causing disruption.

- Malicious insiders can use their privileged access to an organisation's data or networks to conduct malicious activity such as stealing sensitive information to share with commercial rivals.
- With the best of intentions, honest mistakes can sometimes be made by staff. For example, emailing something sensitive to the wrong email address.

What are the Top Threats to Organisations?

Nowadays it is a regular item on news reports that national organisations, utilities and other service providers have been subjected to some sort of online, digital attack of their computerised systems. Often this can be an out and out criminal attack with a view to extorting money but it can also be a more sinister form of asymmetric warfare by one nation state against another. Whilst these attacks can take many and varied forms, we will look at some of the most common which the professional investigator may encounter when advising a client:

- **Phishing.** Untargetted, mass emails sent to many people asking for sensitive information (such as bank details) or encouraging them to visit fake websites.
- **Malware.** Malicious software that makes data or systems unusable until the victim makes a payment.
- **Insider threats.** The potential for damage to be done maliciously or inadvertently by a legitimate user with privileged access to systems, networks or data.

What is Phishing?

Phishing is where you receive an email, message, text or phone call that appears genuine but is actually malicious. Phishing attempts might try to trick you into revealing sensitive information, or may contain a link to a website or attachment that is infected with a virus.

Some attempts are highly random in their approach and can be as simple as the same email being sent to a large number of people in the same organisation. These random phishing emails rely on just one person being sufficiently curious to click on open. Others can be more targeted and may at first glance appear to be from a trusted colleague or company. This type of more targeted attack is known as 'spear-phishing'.

How to Spot Phishing

Traditionally, you were able to spot a phishing email rather easily. Older phishing emails usually contained several giveaways:
- Spelling mistakes.
- Poor grammar, like misusing tenses.
- No familiarity. Instead of using your name, they say 'Sir' or 'Madam'.
- Incorrect email addresses. Instead of John.Smith@gmail.co.uk, an email address could be J0hn.Smith@gmail.co.uk.

These things are obvious when you see them but can still be very easily overlooked. Whilst looking out for any of these giveaways can reveal a phishing email, more modern and targeted spear-phishing emails will often use your real name, good grammar and fake email addresses that look real. This can make them much harder to spot at first glance. There are, however, some key characteristics which you should look out for in any email you consider to be suspicious:

- **The need for urgency.** Using an impending deadline to create a sense of urgency that distracts you from the rest of the message and pressures you into acting quickly. This can involve limited offers, disappearing deals or the promise of enhanced benefits to those who jump in quickly – first come first served.
- **The claim of authority.** Using the authority of the sender, such as pretending to be a more senior staff member, trusted colleague or reliable company, to convince you that the message comes from a trustworthy and authoritative source.
- **Imitation.** Exploiting 'normal' business communications, processes and daily habits to trick you into reacting to a message. Check who the email is addressed to. If it's 'friend' or 'valued customer', this might be because the sender doesn't know you.
- **Your digital footprint.** Whether we realise it or not we all leave a digital footprint. Your digital footprint is essentially anything that you post online that could be found by an attacker. This could be on a professional social media like LinkedIn or something more personal like your Instagram or Facebook.

To minimise your digital footprint, it is important to regularly review your privacy settings so only your friends can view your posts and information. Remember, as a private investigator you will be routinely looking into the private lives of individuals. If they realise that this is being done and by whom, there is nothing to prevent them from turning the tables and looking at your online footprint.

Avoid posting too much specific information about your role online. This can be used by a criminal to enhance their attack by creating a false sense of authenticity about internal systems and processes. Stick to the basics. For example, imagine if you posted online about how good it was to be in a particular office location on the previous day, seeing colleagues you hadn't seen in a while. A perfectly innocuous remark made without a second thought and seemingly harmless. A criminal could make use of that level of detail to add authenticity to their attack because they would know information that surely nobody could know unless they were there also.

Malware

Malware is an umbrella term that covers a range of different threats that are all designed for harming computer systems. It can include viruses, spyware and ransomware. Once it has gained entry to the system, malware can cause damage and disruption to businesses as well as the reputational damage done as a result.

Ransomware encrypts the victim's data or network systems and demands a ransom to restore them. These attacks particularly target businesses which hold personal or commercially-sensitive data and where disruption to business continuity can be more expensive than paying the ransom demanded.

To mitigate the risks from all forms of malware attacks there are simple steps that you can take:

- Ensure back-ups are only connected to devices known to be secure.
- Check back-ups for malware before restoring them.
- Regularly renew products used for back-up.

Insider Threats

Most likely these will come from either current or former employees, particularly if the former employee left under difficult circumstances. Traditional security measures are often designed to protect against external threats rather than internal ones. This means that insider threats can potentially be more difficult to spot. Signs of an insider threat can include:

- Unusual access times logging on to internal systems.
- Accessing resources that are not relevant to the person's role.
- Repeated requests for access to sensitive information.
- Renaming files to disguise their true content.
- Emailing sensitive information to an external recipient.

This list is not intended to be exhaustive, merely illustrative of some of the main ways such threats can show themselves.

Passwords

Passwords can often act as the first line of defence and yet we are probably all guilty of using repetitive or easily-guessed passwords to access the bewildering array of accounts that we all need regular access to.

In this section we will look at password standards, the best ways to create a strong password and the key tips for keeping a password safe and secure. Having a strong password is key to protecting the safety of your account. The question is, what makes a password 'strong'?

- Create separate passwords for critical accounts. Accounts that include critical information about clients, your organisation, evidence of enquiries conducted in sensitive cases and financial information to list just a few. If your accounts are not secure you could be at risk of a cyber incident and, perhaps more importantly, you are also placing your clients at risk.

- Create strong passwords using three random words. Weak passwords can be hacked in seconds. The longer and more unique your password is the stronger it becomes and the more difficult it is to hack.

- Save your password in your browser. It is good practice to use different passwords for the most important accounts. Of course, remembering lots of passwords can be difficult but if you save them in your browser you don't have to.

- Activate 2-step verification (2SV) for your email. 2SV gives you twice the protection so even if cyber criminals have your password they can't access your email. 2SV works by asking for more information to prove your identity. For example, getting a code sent to your phone when you sign in using a new device or change settings such as your password. You won't be asked for this every time you check email.

- Keep your device up-to-date with the latest software to reduce the risk of cyber incidents. This will ensure that all of your devices include the latest security.

- Back up important organisation data and key contacts. This allows you to continue operating even if you suffer a cyber incident. Back-ups can include paper copies, removable media or cloud-based services.

Keep Your Devices Secure

In the previous section we looked at the importance of having strong passwords using at the very least 2SV to keep your important accounts secure. But how do you keep your devices secure?

There are various practices that should be adopted to ensure devices remain secure:

- Removable media refers to items such as USB sticks, CDs and any other form of portable storage that can be plugged into a computer. Removable media is best avoided altogether unless absolutely necessary, cloud-based storage options are much more secure.

- Clear desk, clear screen. Information of value to a criminal does not have to be only electronic data. Post-It notes or other paperwork left lying on a workspace surface can be accessed if the criminal is in the room. Desks and other work environments should always be left clear with papers securely stored away from prying eyes. Likewise screens should automatically lock after a defined period of inactivity and be password protected.

- Downloading apps should only be done from recognised, secure sites. Software from unofficial app stores and websites may contain malware and can cause damage to any device downloading this.

- Insecure Wi-Fi can often be convenient where it is offered free of charge in a public environment, for example, a coffee shop or public space, but can also be very dangerous. Public networks often do not have passwords and can transmit your sensitive data without encryption. This means that a criminal can easily gain access to the information you are sending over that public network.

- Wi-Fi attacks can also happen within your own home, particularly given the increase in people still working from home post-pandemic. The default password provided with your router should always be changed to something more secure.

- All software and apps in everyday use will have weaknesses and flaws. Most developers will issue regular fixes and updates to deal with these as they are identified to help keep your device secure. These updates should be installed regularly. Make it part of your regular routine.

Safe Web Browsing

Malware, scams and other threats can all come from malicious webpages made with the intention of deceiving the unwary browser. To stay safe online, only use HTTPS enabled websites. HTTPS encrypts the data you are sending to any given website and ensures that data received from any such site is legitimate and not intended for criminal purposes. These secure sites can always be identified by the little padlock symbol next to the web address.

Third Party Apps and Warnings

Never install any third-party extensions on to your browser, like adblockers or coupon finders. We have previously looked at the importance of not installing software from unknown sources as these can present the same risks as unknown software and infect you with malware or steal personal or commercially sensitive information. Often in these circumstances you may receive a certificate warning. These should always be taken seriously.

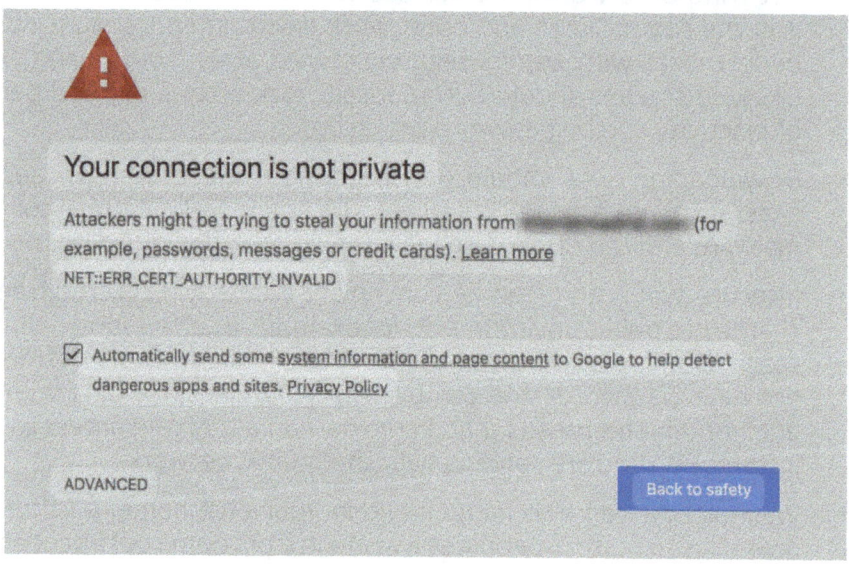

Conclusion

Your device can be exploited both remotely and physically, but by taking the steps outlined in this section, you can help to protect your devices from many of the most common forms of attack by criminals. Here are some key things to remember:

- Keep your software and apps up-to-date with the latest security patches and never ignore an update.
- Be careful to only download apps from official app stores and avoid using unknown or third-party applications.
- Stay with your devices. Never leave them unattended and secure them with a screen lock.
- Be aware of people around you, particularly when on the move.
- Make sure that all websites you use are HTTPS enabled and never ignore warnings.

Stay safe online
Top tips for staff

Regardless of the size or type of organisation you work for, it's important to understand how to defend yourself from cyber attacks.

The advice summarised to the right is applicable to your working life and your home life.

Use strong passwords

Criminals will try the most common passwords (e.g. password1), or use publicly available information to try and access your accounts. If successful, they can use this same password to access your other accounts.

- Create a strong and memorable password for important accounts, such as by combining three random words. Avoid using predictable passwords, such as dates, family and pet names.
- Use a separate password for your work account. If an online account gets compromised, you don't want the criminal to also know your work password.
- If you write your passwords down, store them securely away from your device. Never reveal your password to anyone; your IT team or other provider will be able to reset it if necessary.
- Use 2 step verification (2SV) for important websites like banking and email. 2SV (which is also known as multi-factor authentication or MFA) provides a way of 'double checking' that you really are the person you are claiming to be when you're using online services.

Defend against phishing attacks

Phishing emails appear genuine, but are actually fake. They might try and trick you into revealing sensitive information, or contain links to a scam website or an infected attachment.

- Phishers use publicly available information about you to make their emails appear convincing. Review your privacy settings, and think about what you post.
- Know the techniques that phishers use in emails. This can include urgency or authority cues that pressure you to act.
- Phishers often seek to exploit 'normal' business communications and processes. Make sure you know your organisation's policies and processes to make it easier to spot unusual activity.
- Anybody might click on a phishing email at some point. If you do, tell someone immediately to reduce the potential harm caused.

If in doubt, call it out

Reporting incidents promptly - usually to your IT team or line manager - can massively reduce the potential harm caused by cyber incidents.

Secure your devices

The phones, tablets, laptops or desktop computers that you use can be targeted both remotely and physically, but you can protect them from many common cyber attacks.

- Don't ignore software updates - they contain patches that keep your device secure. Your organisation may manage updates, but if you're prompted to install any, make sure you do.
- Always lock your device when you're not using it. Use a PIN, password, or fingerprint/face id. This will make it harder for a criminal to access a device if it is left unlocked, lost or stolen.
- Avoid downloading fake apps. Only use official app stores (like Google Play or the Apple App Store), which provide protection from viruses. Don't download apps from unknown vendors and sources.
- Cyber attacks can be difficult to spot, so don't hesitate to ask for further guidance or support when something feels suspicious or unusual.
- Report attacks as soon as possible - don't assume that someone else will do it. Even if you've done something (such as clicked on a bad link), always report what's happened.

National Cyber Security Centre
a part of GCHQ

Refresher Check

What is phishing?

A) Where you receive an email, message, text or phone call that appears genuine but is actually designed to steal your passwords or install malware.

B) The activity of catching fish, either for food, hobby or sport.

C) When somebody uses your computer when you're not looking.

What are the three signs of a phishing email, text or call?
- Urgency.
- Scarcity.
- Reciprocity.
- Imitation.
- Authority.

What should you do if you receive a phishing email, text or call?

A) Click the links contained in the message to see if it is legitimate.

B) Reply to confirm you are definitely interested.

C) Report it to Action Fraud by calling 0300 123 2040 or going to www.actionfraud.police.uk or in Scotland through Police Scotland's 101 call-centre.

D) In the case of an email forward it to the Suspicious Email Reporting Service (SERS): report@Phishing.gov.uk.

Recommended Further Reading

National Cyber Security Centre Small Business Guide: Cyber Security

National Cyber Security Centre Information for Self Employed and Sole Traders

National Cyber Security Centre Cyber Security: Practical Tips for Protection Your Organisation Online

There is also a selection of helpful videos on the Local Government Association website that set things out in very clear and simple terms:

https://www.local.gov.uk/our-support/cyber-digital-and-technology/cyber-unpacked

Chapter Ten
Surveillance Law and Procedure

Introduction

With the recent proliferation of mobile phones with ever-better cameras and the miniaturisation of wireless devices capable of transmitting and recording it has never been easier to discretely and covertly record images and sounds of people we are interested in. That said, however, we all also have an inalienable right to privacy and as a professional investigator it is important that you are aware of this and operate within the legal framework. Particularly where you are obtaining evidence which may need to be admissible in court. To be admissible in a court of law the evidence has to have been obtained lawfully but also recorded properly.

In this chapter we will look at the principal pieces of legislation overseeing this important aspect of investigation including the Criminal Procedures Investigation Act 1996 (CPIA), The Human Rights Act 1998 (HRA) and the Regulation of Investigatory Powers Act 2000 (RIPA). Legal considerations around the use of two of the most common forms of surveillance used by private investigators, covert cameras and vehicle trackers, are covered separately in Chapter Eleven.

This subject can be somewhat dry. It is, however, essential for the professional investigator to be able to understand it and apply it particularly when instructed by public bodies or other professional clients such as law firms.

Learning Outcomes

By the end of this section you will:

- Have a better understanding of the key pieces of legislation governing surveillance.
- Have learnt about some of the likely consequences of getting it wrong.

- Understand the difference between directed and intrusive surveillance.
- Have a useful checklist for things to consider prior to conducting covert surveillance.
- Understand the different ways harassment can be committed and when the exemptions can be applied.
- Be aware of the role of the Information Commissioner's Office and useful resources provided by them to assist small businesses.
- Have an improved understanding of the importance of surveillance logs and reports.

The Human Rights Act 1998

The HRA was introduced into law in the UK in 2002 and was borne out of the European Convention on Human Rights (ECHR) which had come into being in 1951 as a response to the crimes committed during the Second World War and the increasing influence of the United Nations.

Even though the UK left the European Union (EU) following the Brexit vote, the European Court of Human Rights is technically part of the Council of Europe, not the EU, and so allegations of human rights breaches can still be dealt with through British courts. There are fourteen Articles under the HRA:

Article 1: Obligation to respect human rights.
Article 2: Right to life.
Article 3: Freedom from torture and inhuman or degrading treatment.
Article 4: Freedom from slavery and forced labour.
Article 5: Right to liberty and security.
Article 6: Right to a fair trial.
Article 7: No punishment without law.
Article 8: Respect for your private and family life, home and correspondence.
Article 9: Freedom of thought, belief and religion.
Article 10: Freedom of expression.
Article 11: Freedom of assembly and association.
Article 12: Right to marry and start a family.
Article 13: Right to an effective remedy.
Article 14: Protection from discrimination in respect of these rights and freedoms.

Article 8

Whilst all of these articles are important, both in their own right and collectively, it is Article 8 that is the most relevant to the work of a private investigator where surveillance forms part of the investigation. Article 8.2 states: *"There shall be no interference by a public authority with the exercise of this right except such as in accordance with the law and is necessary in a democratic society in the interests of national security, public safety or the economic well-being of the country, for the prevention of disorder or crime, for the protection of health or morals, or for the protection of the rights and freedoms of others."*.

Note the legislation refers specifically to public authorities. Strictly speaking therefore the Article 8 protection does not apply to private individuals, including private investigators. However, be under no illusion that as a professional private investigator you will be under the same obligations where you seek to secure and preserve evidence that will be admissible in a court in the UK. If the investigative activity proposed is intended or likely to gather information about the private life of an individual (whether or not that individual is the subject of the investigation) then such activity will fall within the scope of Article 8. *"If the plan is physically to watch an individual in order to observe that individual's movements or associations, or to listen to his or her conversations, or to photograph or video what he or she does, or to deploy a third party to interact with the subject in such a way as to acquire information, or to monitor his or her movements by technical tracking devices, then whether the desired product is to be used for evidential purposes or intelligence purposes, the subject's rights protected by Article 8 will be violated, as will the rights of any third parties present in the surveillance arena."* (Covert Investigation, Sixth Edition, Harfield and Harfield)

Consequences of Investigator Error and Malpractice

There are potentially serious consequences, aside from the professional reputational damage, for any investigators who have not acted properly in the conduct of an investigation where covert surveillance has formed a part. These include:

- A stay in proceedings where investigators are deemed to have unfairly entrapped an offender or enticed an offence that would not otherwise have been committed.
- Exclusion of evidence from trial.

- Becoming the subject of a complaint to either a professional body or even civil litigation.
- Being the subject of averse comment from the Investigatory Powers Commissioner.
- Being subject to disciplinary action for breaching the Police Code of Ethics.

Section 78 of the Police and Criminal Evidence Act 1984 (PACE) provides for the discretionary exclusion at trial of evidence unfairly obtained as follows: *"A court may refuse to allow evidence on which the prosecution appears to rely to be given if it appears to the court that, having regard to all the circumstances, including the circumstances in which the evidence was obtained, the admission of the evidence would have such an adverse effect on the fairness of the proceedings that the court ought not to admit it."*.

For the private investigator, aside from the reasons already listed above, the implications of handing over inadmissible evidence to a client who was relying on that evidence to prove their case are serious indeed. Establish from the outset whether the evidence you obtain on your client's behalf is likely to be required for production in court. If it is then you must ensure you have complied fully with the law.

Since Brexit it has become a common refrain in the UK that politicians propose leaving the ECHR and the HRA and devising a UK-specific Bill of Rights. That may or may not come about and until such time as it does the professional private investigator needs to be comfortable working within the framework of, in particular, the Article 8 protections when engaged in covert surveillance of any kind.

Regulation of Investigatory Powers Act 2000

The Regulation of Investigatory Powers Act 2000 ensures that public bodies have to be accountable for conducting surveillance to avoid breaching a person's human rights. By 'public body' the law is referring to the following:

- Police.
- Security Services, for example, MI5.
- Local Authorities.
- Customs and Excise.
- Environment Agency.
- Royal Mail.
- NHS.

This list is by no means exhaustive but what it does not include is private investigators. Strictly speaking therefore, they do not require authorisation in order to conduct surveillance. However, an important distinction is where a private investigator is conducting surveillance work 'on behalf of' a public body, for example, a local authority. In this case the local authority would still need to obtain a surveillance authority to remain compliant with RIPA and therefore accountable in the event of a miscarriage of justice.

To be accountable, public bodies need to have attempted all other investigative means, sought authorisation from an appropriately qualified person and conducted the surveillance work in compliance with RIPA. Whenever a public body seeks an authorisation, RIPA requires that they adhere to the principles of the HRA. In particular, they will have to justify why they seek to use the powers in terms of legality, necessity and proportionality. The following criteria must be met:

- Is the action lawful?
- Is it necessary?
- Is it proportionate?
- Is the action non-discriminatory?

Under RIPA there are different categories of surveillance – directed surveillance and intrusive surveillance.

Directed Surveillance

Surveillance is directed if it is covert but not intrusive and is undertaken for the purposes of a specific investigation in such a manner as likely to result in the obtaining of private personal information. It is also directed if by way of an immediate response to events or circumstances, the nature of which is such that it would not be reasonably practicable for an authorisation under this part to be sought for carrying out the surveillance.

An authority for directed surveillance may be granted in the following circumstances:

- When needed for a particular case and there are no other means to obtain the evidence.
- In the interests of national security.
- To prevent and detect crime or prevent disorder.
- In the interests of the economic wellbeing of the UK.
- In the interests of public safety.
- To protect public health.
- To assess, collect any tax, duty, levy or other charge payable to a government department.

These, understandably, closely mirror the Article 8 exemptions already detailed at the beginning of this chapter. One important exemption here is when responding to immediate events. For example, if a terrorist incident has just occurred and the suspect is fleeing the scene, it would be in the interests of national security and public safety for CCTV to be quickly utilised in an attempt to locate the fleeing suspect. To not do so whilst seeking an authority would be impracticable and unnecessary. In these same circumstances there would come a point where the immediacy of responding to the situation has passed and an authority may then become appropriate.

Authorisations for surveillance are usually granted by a specially trained and designated authorising officer. In these same circumstances local authorities' applications must be approved by a magistrate.

We have already discussed how private investigators are not 'public bodies' and so do not have to comply with RIPA. However, be aware that where a private investigator is acting on the instructions of a larger organisation or a law firm, there will likely be similar internal processes in place that mirror the RIPA process to ensure best practice is followed irrespective of the narrow requirements of RIPA upon the private investigator.

Intrusive Surveillance

Surveillance is intrusive if it is covert and is carried out in relation to anything taking place on any residential premises or in any private vehicle. It is also intrusive if it involves the presence of an individual on the premises or in a vehicle, or is carried out by means of a surveillance device.

Definition of Residential Premises

"Any premises occupied or used by a person, however temporarily, for residential purposes or otherwise as living accommodation, including hotel or prison accommodation that is so occupied or used. Such accommodation might be in the form of a house, yacht, a railway arch or other makeshift shelter. It includes hotel rooms, bedrooms, barracks and prison cells but not any common area to which a person is allowed access in connection with his or her occupation."

Definition of Private Vehicle

"Any vehicle which is used primarily for the private purpose (family, domestic and leisure use) of the person who owns it or of a person otherwise having the right of use to it. This does not include a person whose right to use the vehicle derives only from having paid, or undertaken to pay, for the use of the vehicle and its driver for a particular journey. A vehicle includes any vessel, aircraft or hovercraft."

Conclusion

Given that private investigators in themselves are not public bodies per se it is clear that there is no de facto requirement upon them to abide by either the HRA or RIPA. However, the reality is more nuanced than this. If you are acting on behalf of a local authority then you will be operating within the HRA and RIPA regime. If you are acting on behalf of a large organisation or a law firm you may be operating within an HRA and RIPA-like regime. At the very least it would be wise to follow the advice of Jenkins (2020): *"In summary I would suggest that you continue with your surveillance as you have been in the past but keep in mind what you would consider as morally acceptable, fair and how you would expect to be treated in the same circumstances.".*

Of course, what is morally acceptable to one person may not be morally acceptable to another. The so-called 'man on the Clapham omnibus' (a hypothetical ordinary and reasonable person) test may not withstand scrutiny by a court. Depending upon the circumstances of the investigation concerned, it may be prudent to apply a more clearly defined set of criteria to ensure that all key issues have been considered by you, as a professional investigator, to take a belt and braces approach.

Checklist for Consideration of Deployment of Covert Surveillance

- What is the evidence or intelligence being sought?
- What is its relevance to the investigation?
- Is this the least intrusive means of obtaining the evidence or intelligence?
- Have we previously attempted to obtain the evidence or intelligence by less intrusive means? If not, why not?
- What is the likelihood of collateral intrusion against the privacy of person(s) not being investigated? How will this be mitigated?
- What are the reputational risks either to myself or my employer by the use of covert surveillance in these circumstances?
- What are the health and safety risks to staff engaged in covert surveillance?
- What are the risks to the public or specific third parties when such tactics are deployed?
- What are the risks to the subject of the investigation?
- Will the proposed methods breach Article 8(1)? If so, is there a justification under Article 8(2) for doing so?
- Will the evidence or intelligence gained as a result of the covert surveillance be admissible in court?

Protection from Harassment Act 1997

This legislation has often been referred to as the 'Stalker's Act' and can encompass a range of circumstances including relationship breakdown, neighbourhood disputes and some cases of domestic violence. For the professional private investigator it could arise where the target of a surveillance operation has become aware that they are being surveilled or, in their terminology, stalked.

There are two criminal offences created by the Act:

1. **Harassment.** Whereby it is an offence to pursue a course of conduct which amounts to the harassment of another when the harasser knows (or ought to know) his conduct amounts to harassment. The offence is arrestable and is dealt with in the Magistrates Court. Upon conviction the sentence is up to six months imprisonment, a fine up to £5,000 or both.

   Note how the offence is only made out by there being a course of conduct. Once is not enough, there must have been two or more *related* occurrences; the conduct does not have to have been violent but it must be 'oppressive' and the conduct does not need to have been the same on each occasion. The fewer the incidents and the greater their separation in time then the less likely it is that they could be described as a course of conduct. Note also how test of 'reasonableness' again is relevant here in that the harasser cannot claim ignorance if they *ought* to have known.

2. **Causing fear of violence.** This is by far the more serious aspect of this legislation and is committed if a person's course of conduct causes another person to fear, on at least two occasions, that violence will be used against him/her. This is triable by the Crown Court to reflect this greater level of seriousness.

There are some obvious exemptions to this as it does not apply to a course of conduct if the person who pursued it shows:

- That it was pursued for the purpose of preventing or detecting crime.
- That it was pursued under any enactment or rule of law or to comply with any condition or requirement imposed by any person under any enactment.
- That in the particular circumstances the pursuit of the course of conduct was reasonable.

It is this latter exemption in particular which may be of assistance to the professional private investigator where it can be shown the 'reasonableness' test applies and where use of the checklist can be useful evidence to support this.

Civil Offence of Harassment

As with any civil proceedings the bar is set lower at the 'balance of probabilities' rather than the 'beyond reasonable doubt' required in criminal proceedings. A civil claim for harassment would be heard in the County Court or in the High Court. Either court can award damages including where it is found the harasser caused anxiety and any resulting financial loss. The victim may also ask the Court to impose an injunction restraining the harasser from pursuing any conduct which is prohibited by that injunction. Breaching this injunction is treated as Contempt of Court and may result in imprisonment for such.

Defence

It is a defence to show that the person's course of conduct was instigated for the prevention or detection of crime, or was authorised by statute, or it was reasonable for the purposes of protecting himself/herself or another person or property. Note how these exemptions closely mirror the circumstances where directed surveillance is justified.

If the Secretary of State certifies that in their opinion anything done by a specified person on a specified occasion related to either national security, the economic wellbeing of the UK or the prevention or detection of serious crime and was done on behalf of the Crown (that is, the country), the certificate is conclusive evidence that this Act does not apply to any conduct of that person on that occasion. Note the crime has to be *serious* crime. Whilst there is no single legal definition of a serious crime in the UK, some factors which are considered include the following:

- **Potential punishment:** where a lengthy prison sentence is more likely.
- **Severity of harm:** where the crime causes significant physical, psychological or financial harm to the victim.
- **Public interest:** where significant public interest exists because of its shocking nature or wider implications.
- **Complexity:** self-explanatory.

Note here that the severity of financial harm, for example, is a relative test not an absolute one. One person may have greater financial losses before the 'serious' threshold is reached whereas somebody else may only need to suffer much smaller losses for the harm incurred to reasonably be termed serious. Also it is always worth remembering, particularly in the context of this piece of legislation that the public interest is not the same as what is of interest to the public. The distinction is an important one to always bear in mind, particularly as a private investigator where you may be conducting surveillance in circumstances where the latter is more relevant than the former.

Data Protection Act 2018

The Act came into force in 2000 and was further revised in 2018 with the introduction of the GDPR. The Act lays out the rules governing the processing of personal data held on some paper records and all electronic data. 'Personal data' relates to the personal information of *living* individuals.

As with most of the content of this chapter dealing with law and procedure, the detail can be very complex and difficult to understand. This chapter therefore is deliberately avoiding getting too detailed. The intention here is to provide the new professional private investigator with an overview of the elements of the essential Acts as it relates to surveillance. Whether you are working as an individual or as part of a registered company, if you are compiling or storing personal data you are required by law to be registered with the Data Protection Registrar.

In addition to the general requirements of the Data Protection Act the introduction of GDPR brought in requirements for data controllers to have a specific GDPR policy in place which specifies how, where and why data is kept and how long it is kept for before being deleted. There are eight enforceable good practice principles which state that personal data must be the following:

1. Fairly and lawfully processed.
2. Processed for one specific and limited purpose.
3. Adequate, relevant and not excessive.
4. Kept accurate and up-to-date.
5. Not kept for longer than necessary.
6. Processed in accordance with the data subject's rights.
7. Unauthorised use or misuse of data prevented by applying acceptable security measures.
8. Not transferred to foreign countries without adequate protection.

Information Commissioner's Office

The Information Commissioner's Office (ICO) oversees regulation of the law in the UK for this important aspect of any business but is of particular importance as a professional private investigator given the intrusive nature of the work at times as well as the inevitable collection and storage of personal data. The ICO website provides a wealth of resources, advice and guidance for small-to-medium-sized enterprises, start-ups, sole traders, small charities, groups and clubs. These tools include an action plan to avoid data breaches, a beginner's guide to data protection and a check to see if data protection requirements apply to your business as well as the inevitable FAQs. (A link to the site is included in the Recommended Further Reading section of this chapter.)

Before conducting any surveillance operation a Data Privacy Impact Assessment (DPIA) should be conducted to risk assess the likelihood of potential breaches before they occur. As stated previously in this chapter, whilst there is no legal requirement upon private investigators to undertake a DPIA, it would be good practice and would further enhance your professional credentials.

Trespass

A trespass occurs when a person directly enters upon another's land without permission, or remains upon the land, or places or projects any object upon the land. It is easy to see how these scenarios could be relevant to private investigators in the course of their enquiries.

The offence of trespass is a civil offence only and not a crime, which is treated as '*de minimis*' – literally '*the law cares not for small things*'. Accordingly private investigators could only be prosecuted through the civil courts. The simple rule to follow is that if you are found to be trespassing on private property and you are asked to leave then leave immediately and without argument. Any owner is within their legal rights to use minimum force necessary in order to remove you or to prevent you from entering. However, this is a scenario to be avoided at all costs.

In practical terms, we have already considered some offences which may be applicable if placing a tracker on a vehicle such as vehicle interference or criminal damage. Where a tracker is placed on a vehicle whilst parked on private land a trespass is committed. Equally however, where that tracker is attached to a vehicle whilst parked on public land the private investigator could still be considered to be interfering with property and therefore committing a trespass.

Bearing in mind the 'de minimis' principle, trespass can be considered to be lawful, proportionate and necessary. In the stated case of 'R v Jackson and others', the Environment Agency (EA) deployed a covert video camera on a target's private property to observe and record activity at the location. The defence accused the agency of committing trespass in doing so. The judge's comments make for helpful reading: "*It follows that I am not satisfied that the placement of the camera or indeed the associated recording equipment amounts to trespass at all. While the EA officers may have momentarily strayed onto the land already identified, that act was so limited in time and degree as to warrant no further consideration. It did not extend beyond doing any more than was necessary to facilitate the surveillance and was entirely incidental to the process of installation of the camera... The trespass complained of was extremely limited, there is no evidence of deliberate wrongdoing, or deliberate contravention of executive powers or guidance. There is a total absence of bad faith.*". (HH Judge John Evans, Newcastle upon Tyne Crown Court, December 2012)

Overall however, this area of activity is one which is so common and so fundamental to the work of the professional private investigator that it is well worth adhering to good practice, laws and procedures even where there is no strict legal requirement to do so. This has already been discussed in the context of RIPA in particular. Whilst the law around trespass is helpful to private investigators, it does not allow 'open season' for whatever action feels expedient and it is important to ensure that only action which can later be justified is considered as part of any investigation.

Surveillance Logs and Reports

As a professional and competent surveillance operative, it is essential that you maintain proper logs and reports. Although it is somewhat of a movie cliche to 'synchronise watches' the point remains valid that all electronic recording equipment and manual records of timings should be accurate as well as consistent with one another. Discrepancies in timings will be seized upon in any future court proceedings and is an obvious pitfall to be easily avoided with the right planning and preparation.

Whilst notes can be recorded on anything it is more professional to record notes on a template designed for such purposes. Ideally surveillance logs should be typed up and submitted along with any accompanying digital evidence and should be in chronological order. Where two or more operatives have worked together there should be no need to produce separate accounts as long as the second operative signs and dates the account produced by the first.

Ideally any notes should be contemporaneous, or as soon as practicable after the events in question. Courts will accept that it is not always possible to be making precisely contemporaneous notes in an active operational setting. However, they should be made soon after whilst events are fresh in the mind. Where a voice recorder is used the recording should be transcribed as soon as possible.

Potentially all information and documentation acquired through covert surveillance is liable to disclosure at trial. The fact that evidence was obtained covertly does not, per se, exempt it from statutory disclosure. There is stated case law on this issue (see R v Sekhorn (1987)). Simply put, the admittance of surveillance logs does not constitute evidence of the facts alleged but does speak to the credibility of the witness relying upon it and can be legitimately used to refresh the memory of the witness who is giving evidence based upon it. It is equally legitimate for other parties to the events described in the surveillance log to make use of that log for the same purposes. So a surveillance log is a useful tool for the witness but falls short of constituting evidence in and of itself.

Completion of Log Book Entries

- For each new surveillance operation a fresh log book should be used.
- The log should commence with a clear statement to the effect that the log keeper identifies themselves and states the name of the surveillance operation, or the reference to the investigation located through whatever system the company uses for such things. The staff involved should be detailed to facilitate the subsequent use of initials in the body of the log.
- The time the surveillance commenced and concluded.
- The detail of what was seen and observed. This can be either by others in the team, if the log keeper has no other role other than to maintain the log, or all involved making use of initials as appropriate without sacrificing clarity.
- Details of any handover of responsibilities during the operation. Such administrative notes within the body of the observation log are perfectly acceptable and complement not only the contemporaneous and authentic nature of the notes but add clarity to the 'ebb and flow' of events as they occur.
- A statement to the effect that the surveillance has completed noting the time.

Debriefing Surveillance Operations

It is good practice to debrief any operation and surveillance is no different. It can be a so-called 'hot' debrief, which is quick, immediate and proximate to the events concerned. It can also be more structured and held some time after the events concerned. Equally it can be both. The important thing is that there is a debrief of some form. The debrief should also be recorded appropriately.

The debrief is conducted in order to identify any discrepancies or inaccuracies that may need to be amended (and recorded as such) in the main body of the log. It also provides an opportunity for additional recollections to be captured and, again, recorded as such. At the conclusion of the debrief the record should be signed and the time noted. These should then be securely stored for future reference.

Refresher Check

There are fourteen Articles under the Human Rights Act. Name five of them.

Of the fourteen Articles, which is the most important for private investigators to consider when conducting covert surveillance?

When a public body seeks an authority under RIPA, what are the four criteria which need to be considered?

The Protection from Harassment Act creates two offences. What are they?

Under the Data Protection Act, there are eight enforceable good practice principles. Can you list four of these?

What does the acronym DPIA stand for?

The offence of trespass is a criminal offence which can be applied to private investigators just the same as any other criminal offence. True or false?

The stated cases law on the submission of surveillance logs as evidence is R v Sekhorn. Can you summarise the findings of this stated case?

At the conclusion of any surveillance operation a debrief should be held. Can you summarise some of the reasons why a debrief is so important?

Recommended Further Reading

'The Theory of Covert Surveillance, The Surveillance Training Course Handbook', Peter Jenkins (2020)

'Covert Investigation' (Sixth Edition, Blackstone's Practical Policing), Harfield and Harfield (2023)

'Surveillance Tradecraft: The Professional's Guide to Covert Surveillance Training', Peter Jenkins (2010)

'Covert Surveillance: The Manual of Surveillance Training', Peter Jenkins (1999)

www.ico.org.uk

Chapter Eleven
Electronic Surveillance

Introduction

In recent years this aspect of surveillance has made huge technological advances in terms of miniaturisation, connectivity, price and quality of imagery produced. Not only that but access to high quality cameras, drones and recording devices has reached the mainstream and can be readily purchased on any high street or platform, such as Amazon. There are no wires, no drilling and storage can be cloud-based making it even easier to bring a wide range of electronic tools to bear on any target for covert surveillance.

The full range of electronic surveillance equipment available to the professional investigator is wider than can possibly be covered here so we will focus on the core elements required to cover most practical scenarios. Whatever equipment is used it should be practical, reliable, easily portable and durable. Maintain it regularly, especially if the kit is not being used all the time. When you need it you need it and anything requiring a power source should be charged and ready to go with spare power as necessary.

Learning Outcomes

By the end of this section you will:

- Have a better understanding of some of the operational benefits of vehicle tracking devices as well as the legal implications of doing so.
- Have learnt more about how such devices work and the common features you can expect to have as tools at your disposal.
- Understand the benefits of covert video cameras as well as the legal implications of when and where they can be used.
- Have learnt more about one of the most recent additions to the toolkit of the professional private investigator – the drone, as well as some of the legal and ethical considerations in doing so.

Vehicle Tracking Devices

Vehicle tracking devices are a much safer and more cost-effective way of keeping tabs on a moving vehicle than attempting a mobile surveillance from another vehicle. There are multiple risks associated with a vehicle follow that simply do not apply when relying on a vehicle tracker device. In recent years trackers have become much more readily available whilst also providing good reliability – usually! Here we look at some common scenarios:

Monitoring Routine Activity

In this scenario a tracker is a particularly cost-effective way to build an intelligence-based picture of the target's movements, daily habits and so on, prior to the deployment of a more costly team of operatives. This is often needed at the commencement of an investigation where this basic level of information is necessary to determine next steps in progressing the enquiry. Most people have regular habits and routines that can be readily discerned if observed over a sufficient period of time. Obtaining this intelligence from a tracker is a useful starting point that can be developed and refined prior to considering next steps.

Monitoring Activity of a Surveillance Aware Target

Where the target may be expecting to be surveilled in some form they may be more likely to conduct anti-surveillance measures – even in a very basic form. In this scenario real-world vehicle follows are particularly high risk if the target decides to drive at high speed to avoid being surveilled. This could place not only the target and the team at greater risk but also presents a risk to members of the public. The safe, cost-effective way to mitigate all of these risks is with a well-placed vehicle tracker.

Total Loss

Where a team of operatives (or indeed a solo operator) has been deployed to conduct the principal surveillance effort, a tracker can prove to be a useful contingency tactic in the event of a loss on the ground. The target can readily be reacquired and the surveillance picked up again.

Providing a Trigger and Retaining Control

If, for example, the target resides in an area where a formal 'trigger' (the person who initiates the follow) could prove risky, a tracker can be deployed to initiate the surveillance until the target can be surveilled more safely using operatives on standby. This option also allows the team to deliberately surrender the 'eyeball' when it becomes expedient to do so to reduce the risk of being compromised. For example, where there are no other vehicles on the road and it would quickly become obvious the target was being followed.

Product Movement Tracking

As well as tracking vehicles, modern devices can be small enough to be discreetly placed within shipments, deliveries and products themselves to track something being shipped anywhere in the world. Obviously such a device would need sufficient power over what may be several days of transportation and connectivity, but these units usually have a low power output and are able to reconnect when a lost signal is resumed.

How Do Tracking Devices Work?

Whilst the range of devices is very large they mostly tend to operate in the same way – by picking up a signal from satellites. Most will read through plastic, wood, glass and fabric but not metal.

Readings are taken from satellites every few seconds and the location co-ordinates are then transmitted via a SIM card over either 4G or GPRS. The frequency of reporting depends on how the device is configured to talk to the main server (usually hosted by the manufacturer) so it requires a phone signal to operate effectively.

The common features of standard trackers includes:

- **Arming.** In 'arm' mode a tracking device can be used as a trigger so as soon as movement is detected it will send a signal alert to tell you it is now moving.
- **Geofencing.** This feature allows the operative to pre-select a defined area (such as a set of streets, a village or even a town) to allow the device to move freely *without* reporting. An alert is only sent once these pre-determined 'geo-fences' are breached.
- **History.** The tracking history between particular dates can be downloaded and saved for later use. This feature is also a useful evidential tool where the data has been properly produced and stored.

There are some basic common sense rules to follow before deploying a tracker:

- Research the type of vehicle you are proposing to follow to determine the best location to place the device.

- Ensure the unit is functioning correctly and fully charged.
- Erase any historical data from the device, particularly important where there is a risk of it being lost or compromised in any way.
- Do not place it near a wheel arch or exhaust.
- Support the magnets where necessary with cable ties.
- Deploy the device whilst in a public space rather than on private property.
- Try to avoid making physical contact with the vehicle as this risks activating an alarm or leaving obvious marks on dirty bodywork.

Use of Trackers: Ethical and Legal Considerations

Tracking devices only provide data on location and, crucially from a legal perspective, not personal or private data. Therefore, Human Rights legislation is not compromised. It can be argued that a tracking device should be considered intrusive surveillance rather than directed surveillance from the perspective of RIPA. However, the Surveillance Commissioner has explicitly stated that the use of trackers (not manufactured or adapted to capture and send an audio or video signal) is not intrusive, provided that the surveillance itself is lawful and no offences are committed in either attaching or removing the tracker (trespass). In effect this means that legally the tracker is treated as a surveillance tool in the same way as a standard single-lens reflex (SLR) camera would be.

Accordingly, information or intelligence obtained from a tracking device should not be viewed as evidence in its own right and should always be corroborated for it to be of evidential value to subsequent court proceedings.

However, Part 3 of The Police Act 1997 states that property interference, entry into or onto any private property (including for deploying surveillance devices) or vehicles trespassing on private land is considered intrusive. Thankfully for our purposes, as the name implies this legislation only applies to police officers and not private investigators!

It has also been suggested that placing a tracker on a vehicle constitutes an offence of 'vehicle interference'. However, this offence comes under the Criminal Attempts Act 1981 which covers situations where a person interferes with a motor vehicle or a trailer (or with anything carried in or on it) which is more than merely preparatory to the commission of a theft.

Therefore if you are deploying a tracking device you are not intending to commit theft.

Another offence to consider would be criminal damage. The Criminal Damage Act 1971 defines someone who causes criminal damage as: 'a person who, without lawful excuse, destroys or damages any property belonging to another, intending to destroy or damages any such property, *or being reckless* as to whether any such property would be destroyed or damaged'. The offence can be proved by showing recklessness so a poorly fitted tracker could fall within this part of the Act.

Covert Video Cameras

Private investigators are able to take videos or photographs in any public space. This includes taking photographs and video of private property whilst they are on public property, for example, a vehicle. Nowadays covert filming is most likely to be through the use of smart phones – everybody has one so they easily go unnoticed. We are all used to seeing people holding them whilst talking into them, perhaps on a video call or just filming for perfectly ordinary reasons. Equally it is very easy to pretend you are taking a selfie whilst actually recording what is in front of you.

Despite the ubiquitous nature of smart phones, there are several techniques you can use to minimise the risk of discovery:

- Take a position where your target is walking towards you. The greater distance you can make use of the better. Many smart phones have limited zoom capability but in the right circumstances this will provide useful identification evidence.
- If you are working as part of a team make use of a colleague as a decoy. Your colleague could be 'posing' for a photograph whilst you are in fact focussed on the target behind them.
- Take multiple shots including background to provide context and cover. This will make it seem less obvious that you are only interested in the environment occupied by the target.

Whilst a smart phone may be the most obvious tool at our disposal, they are not the only one and in recent years covert cameras have become smaller, cheaper and more readily available with enhanced functionality. On the next page there are three covert cameras disguised to look like everyday items: a car key fob, a Bluetooth speaker and a pen. All of these items are available for next day delivery with the most expensive item being under £45.

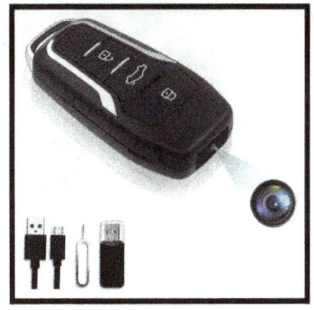  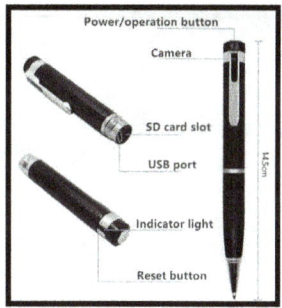

Use of Covert Cameras: Ethical and Legal Considerations

As previously discussed, this area of practice is one where the professional investigator needs to think beyond the narrow confines of what is required by law and take into consideration the wider ethical and reputational challenges use of electronic surveillance presents. This represents both an opportunity and a threat. The stated case to consider in this respect is that of Jones v Warwick (2003). The video footage obtained by the defendant was ultimately admitted into evidence as it went on to disprove the claim. However, the deception practiced by the investigators was deemed by the court to amount to a breach of the claimant's human rights. A useful summary of this case is presented at www.casemine.co.uk.

Summary

Mrs Jean F Jones appeals against an order allowing the defendant, the University of Warwick, to rely on a video film obtained by filming the claimant in her home without her knowledge. The issue is whether a defendant to a personal injury claim is entitled to use such evidence. The court must balance the public interest in revealing the truth in litigation against the public interest in not encouraging unlawful means to obtain evidence.

Facts

The claimant dropped a cash box on her right wrist and suffered a small cut. The defendant used a hidden camera to film the claimant in her home without her knowledge. The defendant's expert concluded that the claimant had satisfactory function in her right hand after seeing the film. The defendant sought directions from the court on the admissibility of the evidence.

Issues

Whether a defendant to a personal injury claim is entitled to use video evidence obtained by filming the claimant in her home without her knowledge after the person taking the film had obtained access to the claimant's home by deception.

Decision

The appeal is dismissed. The court must exercise its discretion when determining the admissibility of evidence. The court must consider whether the evidence is necessary for the protection of the defendant's rights and whether its introduction is in accordance with the law. The court must also deter improper conduct of a party while conducting litigation.

Reasoning

The court must balance the public interest in revealing the truth in litigation against the public interest in not encouraging unlawful means to obtain evidence. The court has a discretion to exclude evidence that would otherwise be admissible. The court must consider the relevant provisions of the Human Rights Act, including Articles 6 and 8. The court must also consider the wider interests of the administration of justice and deter improper conduct of a party while conducting litigation.

England and Wales Court of Appeal (Civil Division) Feb 4th 2003

Drones/Unmanned Aerial Vehicles

Drones, sometimes referred to as Unmanned Aerial Vehicles (UAV), are probably the latest technological innovation to assist the private investigator and have a wide variety of operational uses. Certainly the use of drones is having a major impact on the battlefield but there are plenty of peaceful tasks for these machines to carry out. With their ability to provide a bird's-eye view, drones have quickly become an invaluable asset for private investigators, enhancing capabilities and redefining the way investigations are conducted. They can be used to capture information and intelligence by accessing previously hard-to-reach areas and capture footage from unconventional angles. Equipped with high-resolution cameras, GPS tracking and advanced manoeuvring capabilities, drones have changed the landscape of both covert and overt surveillance. Some of these benefits include the following:

- **Versatility.** Drones can navigate through tight spaces, follow targets discreetly and switch between different locations rapidly,

making them ideal for tracking movements or surveilling areas that are challenging to access by foot.
- **Reduced risk.** In situations where physical surveillance may put investigators in harm's way, drones offer a safer alternative. They can monitor hazardous environments, dangerous individuals or remote locations without exposing investigators to unnecessary risks.
- **Cost-effectiveness.** Traditional surveillance methods often involve a team of investigators and extensive resources. Drones, on the other hand, require fewer personnel and can cover larger areas in less time, reducing operational costs.
- **Real-time monitoring.** Some drones allow for live streaming of footage, enabling investigators to monitor events as they unfold. This real-time access can be crucial for making quick decisions or adjusting the course of an investigation.

In practical terms, private investigators are most commonly involved in cheating spouse investigations, insurance fraud detection and legal case support. Drones are able to monitor a target's movements discretely and record who they may be associating with, provide visual evidence of property damage or accident scenes where a fraudulent claim may have been submitted or obtain evidence of crime scenes and environmental violations such as fly-tipping in a cost-effective and timely way.

Use of Drones: Ethical and Legal Considerations

While drones offer remarkable advantages, their use in private investigations raises ethical and legal concerns. Invasion of privacy, trespassing and surveillance without consent are issues that need careful consideration. Private investigators must adhere to local UK laws, regulations and licensing governing drone use, obtain necessary permissions and respect individuals' rights. As is always the case, professional investigators must ensure that any evidence gathered is admissible in a UK court of law.

Conclusion

As technology continues to evolve, the world of private investigation evolves with it. Drones have opened new possibilities for private investigators, enabling them to gather crucial evidence, enhance surveillance and overcome challenges that were once insurmountable. However, the responsible and ethical use of this technology remains paramount, ensuring that the benefits of drone-assisted investigations are harnessed while respecting individual rights and legal boundaries.

Refresher Check

List three of the scenarios where a vehicle tracking device may prove particularly useful?

What are three of the common features to be found in standard vehicle trackers?

Should a tracking device be considered intrusive surveillance rather than directed surveillance from the perspective of RIPA?

Does placing a tracker on a vehicle amount to an offence of vehicle interference?

What are three of the techniques by which discovery of the use of a smart phone can be made less likely?

Can you describe four of the benefits listed by the use of a drone?

Recommended Further Reading

'*The Theory of Covert Surveillance, The Surveillance Training Course Handbook*', Peter Jenkins (2020)

'*Covert Investigation*' (Sixth Edition, Blackstone's Practical Policing), Harfield and Harfield (2023)

'*Surveillance Tradecraft: The Professional's Guide to Covert Surveillance Training*', Peter Jenkins (2010)

'*Covert Surveillance: The Manual of Surveillance Training*', Peter Jenkins (1999)

Chapter Twelve
Static Surveillance

Introduction

Conducting effective static surveillance is a core function of any professional private investigator and one which requires patience and planning. Static surveillance could be a standalone task or an element within a wider surveillance operation which is at times both highly mobile and static (often for prolonged periods of time). Where it forms part of a wider operation with multiple phases, it is vital the professional operative is able to resume swiftly as well as move between different phases without compromise.

Learning Outcomes

By the end of this section you will:

- Have a better understanding of what a static observation post (OP) is and the types of vehicles, premises and locations which make for a good OP.
- Be aware of important considerations when selecting an OP, including the advantages and disadvantages of urban and rural locations.
- Understand the importance of a recce of any potential OP before deployments by either yourself or your team.
- Know about the important case law regarding the use of OPs.

Static Observation Posts

A static observation post can be many things depending upon the nature of the operation. It can be: a vehicle; a building; natural cover, such as undergrowth; even just in plain view, such as a bus stop where you will not draw attention upon yourself. They can be urban or rural, short-term or long-term.

Vehicles

Using a vehicle as an OP has many advantages. For example, if using your own vehicle it can be convenient and cheaper. Any vehicles, obviously, also allows for rapid transition into a mobile phase if the target moves off. There are also additional benefits such as a source of heat and a radio for longer periods of inactivity – although, of course, this should not be at the expense of paying attention! A vehicle also provides capacity for the storage of equipment and a stable platform for taking photographs or other recording options.

Depending on the nature of the vehicle it may also be possible to use an element of subterfuge to further mitigate the risk of being discovered. For example, a van can be easily made to look like a trade van with the application of magnetic signage. For longer stints it can be a good investment to ensure operatives have a reasonable physical environment in which to spend periods of time, sometimes in inclement weather or where boredom can be a challenge to overcome. A vehicle with insulation from excessive heat, cold or noise and some home comforts thrown in would make any extended period of surveillance much easier to bear.

Despite these obvious benefits there are also clear drawbacks to the use of a vehicle as an OP. These include the following:

- Remaining static for lengthy periods of time in one place may draw attention to the vehicle.
- Parking restrictions can limit the options when selecting the optimum place to park.
- Tinted windows afford privacy but can also make a vehicle look suspicious.
- Any vehicle can ultimately be identified by the registration plate.
- The overall appearance of a vehicle can make it look out of place if it is either too shabby or too smart for the locality it's deployed in. Any vehicle needs to 'look right'.

Clearly selecting an appropriate location is crucial and wherever possible this should be recce'd beforehand. Consider not only the location which provides the best line of sight to the target but also affords adequate means of extraction if the OP might need to become mobile. Alternatively an extraction might be where the risk of compromise has become too great to contemplate remaining in situ. Residential streets will naturally provide good cover although may also draw attention to an unusual vehicle parked in the street. This is less so on an industrial estate where vans in particular will come and go more frequently with less likelihood of being noticed.

As with any surveillance scenarios it is a good idea to have a 'back story' if challenged by somebody as to why you are there. The last thing an operative wants is to draw attention to themselves by attracting attention from an observant member of the public, even less so if that generates a call to the police of a suspicious vehicle. Having a marked police car turn up is guaranteed to compromise the operation. Be clear beforehand what your reason for being there is. Are you waiting for a friend? Have you broken down? Are you waiting to go in to a nearby dentist's for an appointment? This is where a recce beforehand will stand you in good stead.

Other considerations when selecting a suitable location include whether the target would have to drive or walk right past you when they become mobile. If you are in a cul-de-sac, for example, this may be inevitable but not desirable. If there is a likelihood of your vehicle having to transition from a static OP to a mobile resource, is it parked facing the likely direction of travel or will time be lost performing an awkward (and very obvious) three-point turn? Are you likely to have your line of sight obstructed regularly, for example, by delivery vehicles where there is a busy commercial premise nearby? All of these considerations and risks can be effectively mitigated during a recce wherever this is possible.

A final consideration when deploying vehicles into any surveillance operation, but particularly a static surveillance, is that the overuse of one particular vehicle will increase the risk of compromise. Even without being particularly suspicious people will eventually notice if one particular vehicle regularly seems to be 'popping up' within their local environment. Use sparingly and wherever possible rotate. This is not always practical but could nonetheless form part of any risk assessment beforehand.

Ultimately you can only reduce the risk of compromise, not remove it altogether. Sometimes these factors are within our own control, such as:

- Choosing the most appropriate position.
- Not making unnecessary movement or noise whilst inside the vehicle.
- Not allowing equipment, such as a camera lens, to be seen.
- Avoiding a 're-supply' run which draws attention to the OP.

Equally some factors are beyond the control of even the most thoroughly thought through OPs, such as inquisitive children or dogs. In any event if you have considered the extraction, it is always better to remove yourself than risk the welfare of operatives or the compromising of the operation itself.

Buildings

Buildings provide a natural location for an OP in both urban and rural environments and can include structures such as derelict buildings, caravans, hotel rooms, offices, residential properties and other outbuildings. There is important case law to be considered before the use of any private premises which we will come to later in this chapter (R v Johnson 1988 and R v Rankine 1986 in particular) but choosing the most appropriate building will require some pre-planning and forethought.

Advantages of using a well-chosen building include many of those already detailed above: protection from the elements; a stable platform to enable recording of still or moving images from a camera; possible toilet or other facilities for staff engaged in lengthy observations; discretion; an ability to store equipment to allow easy access when needed; access to a power supply to recharge equipment when necessary. Some other considerations when selecting a suitable OP within any type of building include the following:

- Ease of ingress and egress. This should be discreet and secure to allow for changes of personnel, replenishing and rapid evacuation in the event of a potential loss of cover.
- Good line of sight to the target to enable effective recording of images.
- Be aware of potential for silhouettes against a lighter background.
- Check for internet access.

Issues such as resupply should be able to be greatly mitigated by effective planning before the event. However, there are always unforeseen circumstances where this need may occur. Secure your route in and out.

In more rural areas the selection of any OP, whether vehicle or building, can be a challenge. The more remote the location, the fewer vehicles and buildings there will be to blend in with.

Covert Rural Observation Post

Covert Rural Observation Post (CROP) is a surveillance technique that involves blending into rural surroundings to make covert observations. CROP officers undergo rigorous training that includes learning how to construct observation posts, use night navigation and remain self-sufficient for up to 48 hours. In both the military and the police service, this aspect of surveillance is a highly specialised role.

As a professional private investigator the advice would be to avoid this option unless absolutely necessary. Without being properly trained, the risks of discovery are too high and will more often outweigh the potential benefits. Very few, if any, of the benefits already detailed in this chapter apply in this scenario. This method will usually entail long periods of discomfort and inactivity, in potentially challenging weather conditions.

However, if there really is no other option but to conduct surveillance from a rural OP some considerations include the following:

- Ensure you have adequate food and drink, including hot drinks.
- Toilet paper!
- Sufficient batteries and/or battery packs to keep equipment charged and ready for use.

R v Rankine 1986 QB861

Two police officers, with the assistance of an image intensifier, observed the accused from a distance of some 65 yards. They radioed a description of what they observed to another officer who arrested the accused for supplying cannabis. It was the prosecution's case that on ten occasions in the previous hour the accused had been observed selling drugs outside a shop. In the absence of the jury, the prosecutor sought a ruling that the police officers should not be asked questions that would identify the location of the observation post. The application was made on two grounds: firstly, the OP would lose its utility if its location became known; secondly, it was felt that persons who had provided the OP would, or could, be placed in jeopardy from persons who disapproved of co-operation with the police.

The judge ruled that he would not compel officers to answer questions to which they objected on the basis that the answers might embarrass the sources of co-operation. The accused was convicted and appealed on the grounds that the judge was wrong in law in permitting the prosecution not to disclose the OP from where the identification was made.

Dismissing the appeal, the court recited the authorities which had established the very clear principle that the identity of informants who assist the police should not be disclosed unless non-disclosure would result in a miscarriage of justice. The question to be determined was whether this rule extended to protect the identity of those who had allowed their premises to be used for surveillance and the identity of the premises themselves.

In the court's judgment, the reasons which gave rise to the rule applied with equal force to the identification of the owner or occupier of the premises used for surveillance, and to the identification of the premises themselves. The judge had been correct in not exercising the duty exceptionally to admit the evidence in relation to the OP in order to avoid a miscarriage of justice.

> This case needs to be read in the light of the later case of *R v Johnson [1988]*. In addition, the case confirmed that the general rule is indeed a rule of exclusion with a duty to admit the evidence if necessary to avoid a miscarriage of justice. The judge did not have a discretion in the matter. Even if the prosecution do not invoke the rule, the judge is obliged to apply it.

Getting In and Getting Out

Because of the likely more isolated nature of a rural OP, ingress and egress without compromise is even more important and a pre-deployment recce is essential. If the OP is in an isolated building, consider how a vehicle can approach safely and operatives going in to the OP can safely unload both themselves and equipment from the vehicle. If the vehicle is to remain in situ can it do so without fear of compromise? If it is leaving the area once the team has been dropped off consider whether that is also suitable for an emergency rendezvous. It may be that an alternative location should be used for picking up than for dropping off to reduce the risk of attracting unwelcome attention with the increased comings and goings. This level of attention to detail can make or break a successful deployment into any OP but particularly a more rural OP and a thorough risk assessment, as always, should form the basis of your pre-deployment planning.

Protection of OPs

The case law in this regard is very clear and should be well-known to the professional private investigator in the same way as it is a core element of police professional practice. Failing to adequately protect OPs, and those living in or owning them, is likely to seriously impede investigations when they get to court. The threshold here is set at the same level as that provided for the protection of human sources of information – specifically that the identity of locations used as OPs should always be safeguarded unless doing so would lead to a miscarriage of justice.

The other significant piece of legislation, already referred to in this chapter as well as the judgement in Rankine is that of R v Johnson and later confirmed by R v Hewitt and Davis (1992) 95 Cr App R 81 and R v Grimes (1994) Crim LR 213.

Whilst the procedural requirement set out in the case law above clearly applies to police officers it should not be lost on the professional private investigator that as with much case law regarding surveillance (such as Article 8 of the Human Rights Act) there should nonetheless be a compelling case for private investigators to pay close heed to these rulings and to incorporate these actions and considerations into their own professional practice, whether explicitly required to by law or not.

Harfield and Harfield go on to state: "*Because exposure of unmarked police vehicles would not necessarily involve the same threat of harassment or fear of violence that members of the public who make premises available for OPs might face (Blake & Austin v DPP (1993) 97 Cr App R 169), the same presumption of protection would not, as a matter of policy, be applied to police vehicles from which observations were conducted (R v Brown and Daley (1988) 87 Cr App R 52). It therefore follows that vehicles and any other OP used by professional private investigators should adhere to the principles laid out in Rankine and Johnson.*".

R V Johnson (1988) 1 WLR 1377

The criteria set out in this case are reproduced in the ACPO Practice Advice on Core Investigative Doctrine (2005) 104 which states:

The police officer in charge of observations of a rank not lower than Sergeant must be able to testify that beforehand he or she visited all of the observation places to be used and ascertained the attitude of the occupiers of the premises:

- as to the use of the premises
- as to the disclosure of the use of the premises
- to the possible identification of the premises or the occupiers
- to the difficulties, if they are encountered, in obtaining observation posts in the area.

In addition, immediately prior to any trial, an officer of the rank not lower than Chief Inspector, must be able to testify that he or she visited the premises used for observations and ascertained if the occupiers are the same as when the observations were conducted and, whether they are or not, what their attitude is to the:

- possible disclosure of the use of the premises
- disclosure of facts which would lead to the identification of those premises and their occupiers.

This evidence will be given in the absence of the jury when the application is made to exclude the material evidence. The judge should explain to the jury the effect of his or her ruling regarding the disclosure of the premises.

Source: ACPO Practice Advice on Core Investigative Doctrine (2005) as reproduced in Blackstone's Covert Investigation, Sixth Edition, Harfield and Harfield, 2023

Static Surveillance in Urban Environment

Setting

Cotswold Private Investigations (CPI) was hired by an insurance company to surveil Mr X, a construction worker claiming a debilitating back injury. The case requires CPI agents to conduct a 12-hour static surveillance shift from their vehicle near Mr X's private residence in a quiet suburb.

Setup

Two CPI agents arrived at 05:30 hours, parking their unmarked silver Ford Focus two streets over from Mr X's terraced house. They deliberately chose a spot with sight-lines to both the front door and the alleyway leading to a rear parking lot. Equipment available to them included binoculars, a DSLR camera with a 300mm lens, a dash cam, a thermos of coffee, and protein bars. In case of a foot surveillance becoming necessary both agents were wearing neutral-coloured casual clothing to avoid attention.

Surveillance Day

06:00 hours-08:30 hours: Mr X remained indoors. The CPI agents remained in the static surveillance position, using a discreet car blanket to hide the camera. A short while later Mr X exited the premises, limping noticeably, and entered his car. The CPI agents started filming using their dash cam but lost sight when he abruptly turned into a narrow alley blocked from their view.

09:00 hours: the CPI agents took the risk of repositioning their car, circling the block to find Mr X's vehicle parked outside a local gym. Using the DSLR they captured clear footage of him lifting weights without difficulty.

10:30 hours: returning home, Mr X resumed his limp. This change in his behaviour was fully documented. After a further 90 minutes of static observations a neighbour knocked on the window of the agents' vehicle, questioning their presence. Having previously prepared a cover story the CPI agents were able to reply that they were council staff surveying parking availability as part of a consultation for local residents' parking permits. This effectively defused suspicion by reassuring the neighbour.

Outcomes

The evidence obtained by the CPI agents (photos of Mr X at the gym and detailed notes with dates and times clearly recorded) was sufficient to expose the fraud. The insurer denied Mr X's claim, citing deliberate misrepresentation.

Lessons Learned

Location reconnaissance. The agents' initial location to park up missed the alley's exit. Pre-surveillance reconnaissance of all potential routes and alternate vantage points is critical and this could have been better and more thorough. Fortunately the target was quickly reacquired.

Application. Use maps/local knowledge to identify choke points and ensure visibility of all exits. These had been used but not as thoroughly as they should have been.

Cover story. The interruption by the neighbour was a foreseeable risk. The agents had successfully anticipated this and prepared a suitable cover story which proved useful on the day. The story used was very believable given the local surroundings where parking amongst local residents is an issue.

Wellbeing and alertness. Given that it was not possible to determine how long the agents would need to be in the static surveillance vehicle, they had sensibly planned for some additional comforts – a thermos flask for hot drinks as well as snacks. The use of a vehicle also provided a source of warmth, entertainment in the form of the radio and shelter from any inclement weather.

Evidential requirements. The use of a professional DSLR camera allowed for the necessary evidential-quality photographs to be obtained. They were also date and time stamped effectively proving the case against Mr X. This was further supported by the contemporaneous notes of the CPI agents.

Conclusion

Success hinged on adaptability and thorough evidence collection, but the close call with the neighbour and initial blind spot underscored the need for meticulous planning. Static surveillance balances patience with strategic foresight – every detail, from tech to backstories, must be airtight to avoid compromise.

Refresher Check

A static location from which to conduct surveillance is referred to as an OP. What does OP stand for?

There are many advantages to using a vehicle as an OP. Can you list four of them?

There are, however, also several drawbacks to using a vehicle as an OP. Can you list four of them?

List as many things as you can that should be considered before deploying in a vehicle as a static OP.

Before using private premises as an OP, what are the two important stated cases which should be considered before a deployment?

The acronym CROP refers to surveillance training undertaken by military and police personnel. What does CROP stand for?

List some of the factors to consider when deploying to any OP, but particularly to a rural OP.

Recommended Further Reading

'The Theory of Covert Surveillance, The Surveillance Training Course Handbook', Peter Jenkins (2020)

'Covert Investigation' (Sixth Edition, Blackstone's Practical Policing), Harfield and Harfield (2023)

'Surveillance Tradecraft: The Professional's Guide to Covert Surveillance Training', Peter Jenkins (2010)

'Covert Surveillance: The Manual of Surveillance Training', Peter Jenkins (1999)

Chapter Thirteen
Foot Surveillance

Introduction

A lot of intelligence can be gained when out on foot. However the exposure risk is high and self-confidence is a very important factor. A foot surveillance carried out single-handedly can be risky over long periods of time so a minimum of two operators is recommended. A good standard of foot surveillance by an operator or team can only be acquired by practise and experience.

Difficulties can occur if there is a lack of communication between the team. You need good equipment and your radio commentary has to be precise.

Learning Outcomes

By the end of this section you will:

- Understand the basic principles of the A, B, C method of foot surveillance.
- Have better awareness of important considerations when engaged in following a target in a range of different environments.
- Understand some of the tactics to deploy during an active follow.
- Be able to minimise the risk of detection.
- Be more familiar with terminology used to describe the location and movement of the target in a range of different environments.
- Be more confident in deploying in a smaller team adapting to the A, B method where necessary.

The Surveillance Operator

The ideal operator could be described as being the 'grey person'. Someone who does not put themselves above the baseline by the way they dress or the way they act. There are three things that will always get you noticed:

1. Multiple sightings.
2. Unnatural behaviour.
3. Cross contamination.

We will now look at these three aspects of our behaviour in more detail as each is of equal importance to the effective conduct of foot surveillance.

Multiple Sightings

It is obvious that the more times a target sees you increases the chances of them remembering you. You will always be seen but being noticed is something different and being noticed is what you are trying to avoid. Wherever you are you should try to avoid entering the "10 to 2" arc of vision.

You should remain to the side or behind the target at all times. If you find yourself in a situation where you do get in front of the target get out of the way as soon as possible.

Unnatural Behaviour

It is easier said than done but we have to act naturally and have a reason for being there in everything we do. It takes practise to 'act normal', not to talk noticeably into your sleeve, constantly touch your earpiece, shift about or peer around corners. Keep it simple. Take a look around you, fit in with everyone else in the environment because every situation and place will be different. Don't forget to dress according to the car you drive. Being dressed in 'scruffs' and driving a new BMW will get you noticed.

Cross Contamination

Strictly speaking, you should never meet up with another team member unless it is essential. If the target suspects you are surveilling them, he will keep a subtle watch on you to see what you do. If you then speak to another team member you will also compromise them by what we call 'cross contamination'. The target's interest will now switch to the other team member. You should also be aware that a more sophisticated target may employ counter-surveillance and it is these people that will be looking for you. You do not want to make their job easier by compromising the rest of your team.

On training courses, we often use targets that are unknown to the team and who have never seen the students before. This provides good feedback to the class in order to establish their 'exposure' levels and whether the target has identified them. The class are always briefed that those remaining outside of the target's '10 to 2' arc will be most likely to avoid detection. When it comes to the debrief, those noticed by the target are always those who were in the '10 to 2' arc.

Foot Surveillance Tactics

Trigger Positions

The following street plan represents a generic, basic street layout that could be found in any of the towns and cities up and down the country. For the purposes of this module, we are starting with the target located in the bar and represented by the orange star with no letter identifier. We will also assume that there are no rear exits to the bar so our target can only leave via the front door.

Position A

Being right outside the only exit from the premises has both advantages and disadvantages. With a bus stop immediately outside the bar an operative can loiter without being noticed. It would not seem suspicious to allow more than one bus to go past. Being so close to the target will allow for good identification when they leave and reduces the likelihood of any sudden departure being missed altogether.

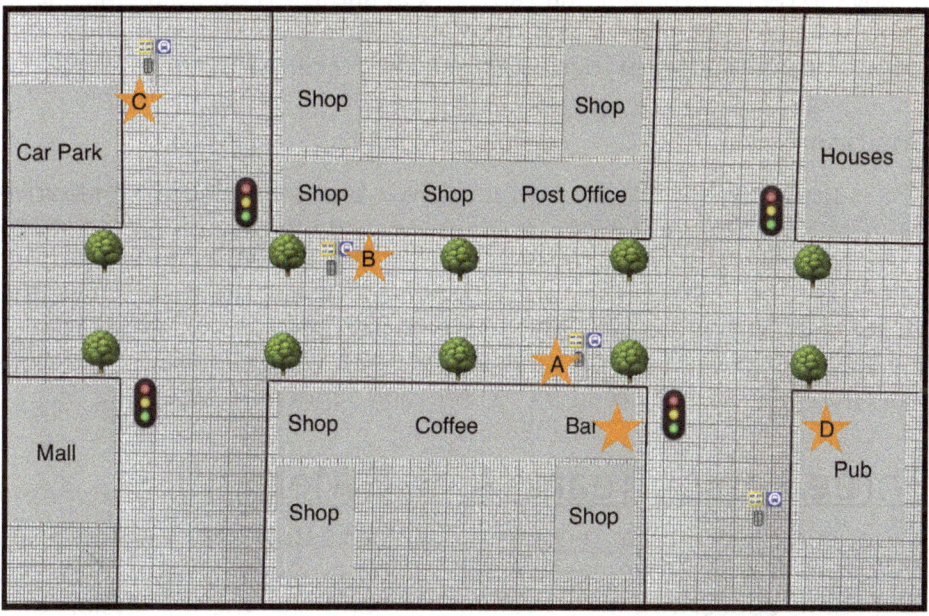

There is also good line of sight with other team members. An obvious disadvantage, however, is the increased risk of being noticed if there is anything unusual about your demeanour or anything else that makes you stand out, particularly if you are as close again during later phases of the surveillance, whilst you are in the '10 to 2' arc.

Position B

This position makes effective use of the bus stop. Even if the operative is the only person standing at the stop it should not draw attention and allows good line of sight of the only exit from the target premises. At least to start with it is also outside of the '10 to 2' arc and if the target turns right upon exit this position remains effective for a follow. A possible disadvantage could be where the street scene is busy with multiple pedestrians and vehicular traffic obscuring not only a clear view but also impeding free movement in the event of the target moving. With traffic lights in the vicinity, a high-sided vehicle could become stationary for several minutes obstructing the view.

Position C

This position makes good use of the bus stop and is outside the '10 to 2' arc. It also provides a degree of forward planning should the target exit the premises and turn left as it places an operative ahead of the target but with the flexibility to pick up the lead in more than one direction. A potential disadvantage may come if the target exits and turns right, in which case the operative at position C will need to be firmly in the communications loop to be able to stay in touch sufficiently to take over when needed.

Position D

This is probably the tasking everybody wanted! Assuming the operative has a window seat with a view outside they are well outside of the '10 to 2' arc and able to stay in situ for as long as may be required with all their comforts provided for. They are well-placed for any situation where the target exits and turns right, whichever road is then subsequently taken. If the target exits the bar and turns left the operative in position D is well-placed to pick up at the rear of the team and support as necessary.

Three Person Team (A, B, C Method)

A foot surveillance team requires mobility and frequent changing of its operators in order to prevent compromise. In diagrammatic form, the formations appear to be very regimented and give the impression that these positions must be strictly adhered to. This is not so because when on the ground an experienced operator will take up his position without thinking. The use of three people in a team permits greater variation in the positioning of the operators and also allows for a member who may be getting 'warm' to be replaced by someone else. It reduces the risk of losing the target and affords greater security against standing out. Whether you are deploying a three person team or a two person team (more likely in the commercial world) all of these principles still apply equally.

Phase 1: The Stakeout

The trigger should be in a position close enough to identify the target but far enough away not to be seen whilst remaining outside of the '10 to 2' arc. He needs to carry out a radio check with the other team members and ensure they are in position and ready to take the follow. If nothing is happening and you may be in for a long wait, the trigger should come up on the radio and report 'no change, no change' on a regular basis. It lets the team know that nothing has happened and acts as a radio check, giving confidence to the rest of the team. On a surveillance radio network there is nothing worse than long periods of silence. If nothing is heard, operators start to fiddle with the radio to see if it is still working and possibly move position to see what is happening, so keep the team informed at regular intervals!

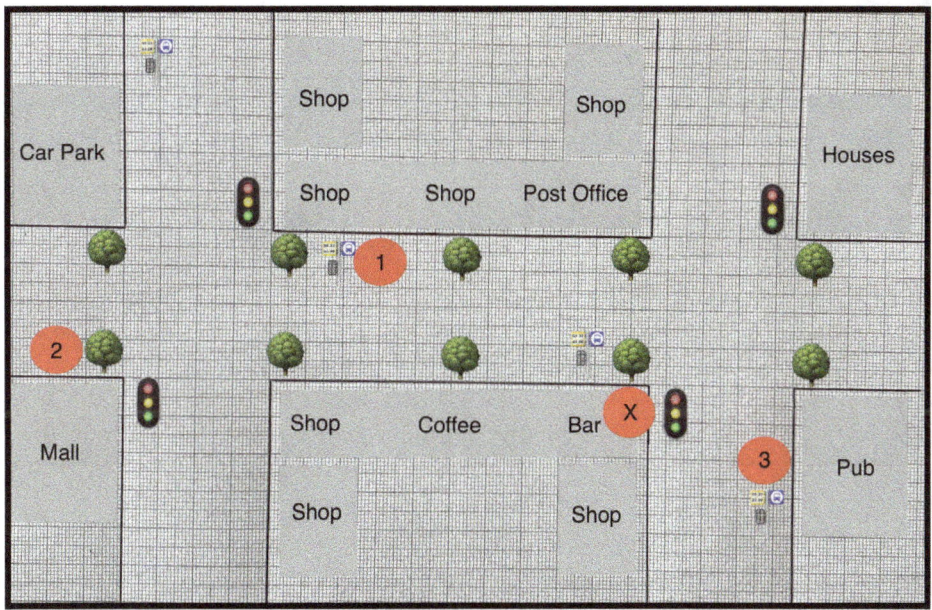

Phase 1: The pickup starting deployments.

Phase 2: The Pickup

When the target appears the 'eyeball' should immediately call 'standby, standby'. This is a wake-up call to the team to say 'let's go' and listen in to the commentary. The eyeball should give a direction of travel and a brief description.

Between the three operatives now in the field with the target, it is important that communication between them is maintained, is succinct and they work together as a team to maintain eyeball, taking turns as necessary and circumstances allow to reduce the risk of compromise.

We say that there are no rules in surveillance but a very important guideline is that the trigger person never moves on a standby (unless as a last resort) to take the first follow.

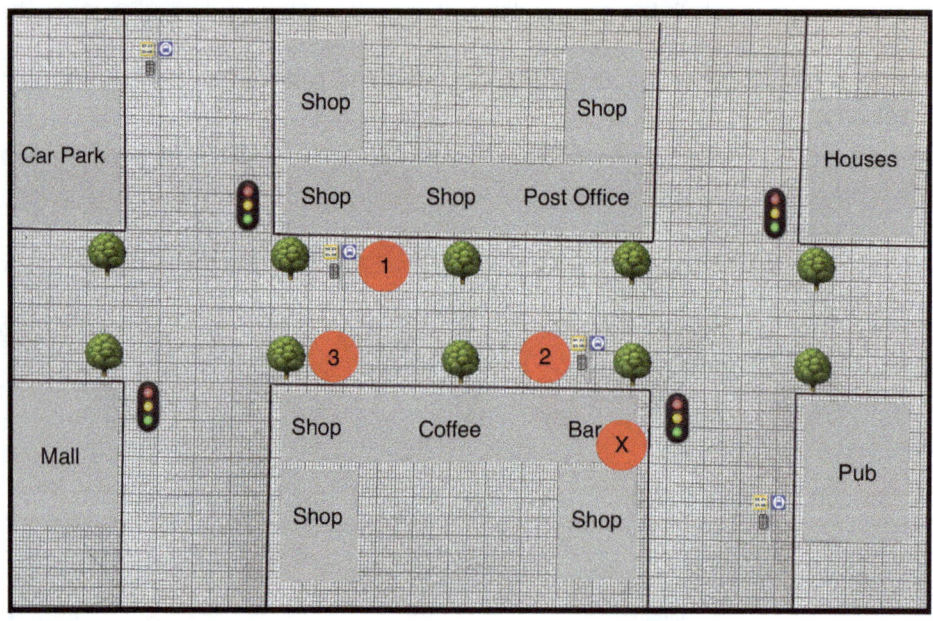

Phase 2: The follow starting deployments.

Phase 3: The Follow (and Housing)

As soon as practically possible the surveillance team will filter themselves into the most appropriate positions to maintain the follow. For example, where Foot 2 has the eyeball, he positions himself behind the target at a safe distance (depending on the area and amount of people) and provides a running commentary. Foot 3 is the back-up and positions himself behind the eyeball, also at a safe distance. It is not necessary for the back-up to see the target. Foot 1 is the trail position and takes up position on the other side of the street. The team is now positioned in what is called the classic A, B, C formation. This formation is not set in stone. The building block of foot tactics is dependant upon the area, the size of the team and the awareness level of the target.

Distancing Rule of Three

In order to judge how close or how far away you should be from the target and each other you have to consider the target's pace, your own pace, the cover that is available and the distance he is away from you. Plus whether there are any changing situations such as transferring from a busy crowded shopping mall into a quiet side-street.

As a rule, you should look at the area and try to be three people distance apart. So in a very crowded place where everyone is bunched up you would be close together. Whereas in a more open area you would be further apart as shown in the diagrams.

Impose Surveillance

If the target crosses from the near side of the street to the offside (left to right) the eyeball and back-up should not follow. This is why we 'impose' surveillance on a target rather than 'follow' the target. Foot surveillance is about team work and communication. If you lose sight of the target we use the term 'temporary unsighted' so that another team member can take control if need be. We've mentioned the importance of staying out of the '10 to 2' arc. You also need to bear in mind that if the target turns around you don't want to be in direct view. Don't dive in and out of cover. Street furniture can provide temporary cover from view, such as other pedestrians, advertising boards, lampposts, shop doorways and parked cars. On the street you have to make constant appraisals regarding the target's intentions and always think to yourself what if he stops, crosses the road, enters a building or turns around? If you are operating in a pedestrian precinct, keep to the sides so that you can easily enter a shop if the target turns around.

Be aware of other body language traits. If the target walks to the outside of the pavement expect them to cross the road, or if they walk into the pavement they may be about to enter a building. Someone constantly looking at their watch could have an appointment or meeting. Searching or patting their pockets indicates they are looking for something and an increase in speed following a phone call might indicate activity.

In very crowded streets the A, B, C method can be difficult to adhere to. There may be times when it is necessary for all three operators to be on the same side of the street as the target. If you are close to the target do not allow your radio commentary to be overheard.

A street with little or no traffic, such as a housing estate, can create challenges. It may be that only one operator is on the same side of the street as the target with the two other operators opposite or perhaps only one operator is deployed if the area is quiet. If a vehicle is used as back-up, a foot operative can be picked up and re-deployed ahead of the target if needed.

Change of Eyeball (Handover)

The closer the operative is to the target the more likely being seen and noticed will become. This makes it imperative that there are regular handovers to minimise the risk of compromise. In the absence of a clear sign that there has been a compromise, it can otherwise be a question of judgment as to whether a handover would be expedient. Handovers should be considered when:

- You have had 'eyeball' for some time.
- The target changes direction.
- The target stops.
- You're compromised.
- The target is lost to view.

Obviously the larger the surveillance team is, the more frequent handovers can be. However, realistically, it is more likely that you will be working in a team of two or three. Handovers should be done only when necessary.

The Target Performs a U-Turn

The target's body language can be a good indicator of imminent behaviour. Try to avoid looking startled or provoked into unusual responses in the event of a u-turn. Most importantly, avoid accidental eye contact. If you have radio communication with the rest of the team you should have a pre-arranged signal to indicate a u-turn. Alternatively a pre-arranged word which can be said without moving your lips. Whatever the protocol, the key is to anticipate and avoid surprise.

Action on a Stop (Housing)

During a follow, if the target then enters a building we have moved from the follow phase into the latter part of that phase – housing. This is an opportunity to reset the team into an optimum configuration, perform any handover as necessary and ensure things like communications are still effective. Team welfare is also an important factor to consider when the target is housed. This is not a rest period. Think about the overall aims and objectives of what you are trying to achieve. Are there any exits that will need securing and, last but not least, is a visual containment from outside the premises sufficient or is there a reason to enter the building with the target.

Phase 2, the pickup, can begin very quickly so it is important to run through these considerations in a timely manner with a trigger person tasked to the door of the premises or indeed any exit where the target may leave from.

Building with Multiple Exits

If the target goes into a building with another exit or is located on a street corner, the eyeball on handing over should overshoot and at the same time check the rear and side for possible additional exits. If there are multiple exits the rest of the team need to be appraised and triggers allocated to secure each one.

To ensure accuracy of communications, it is common practice to use the face of a clock to designate direction. For example, if a target goes into a building the point of entry is always at 6 o'clock. If there is then a potential means of exit on the right hand side this would become an exit at 3 o'clock in need of securing.

Cafes and Pubs

If the target goes into a cafe or a pub, you must decide whether to follow inside or remain outside and place a visual containment on the premises. Whatever you decide here will be based upon several external factors particular to the circumstances of the investigation (for example, is the target likely to be meeting someone?) or the physical topography of the building (for example, is there an exit that you are unable to adequately cover?). Consider also whether by going in you will be drawing attention to yourself to such an extent that it will make it very difficult to then maintain a foot follow without being noticed. Some points to remember:

- Do not feel awkward in public places. You are a member of the public so are entitled to be there.
- If you choose to go in, always have a cold drink. If the target suddenly leaves it may seem odd if you leave a hot drink or meal on the table.

- Pay for any beverages as you order them. You do not want to be delayed leaving by waiting to settle up a bill if the target leaves unexpectedly.
- Sit close if a meeting is taking place. You do not have to be facing a target to overhear what may be being discussed.
- Make good use of your mobile phone. It is commonplace to see people staring and scrolling on their phones nowadays. You can be updating the team whilst not drawing attention to yourself. Make sure, however, that your phone is on silent mode so as not to draw unnecessary attention to yourself.

Shopping Centres

These can usually be treated in the same way as a street, the principles are the same. Some additional considerations, however, will include the likely presence of security guards and increased level of CCTV. If you act unnaturally you are more likely to be tracked from their CCTV control room.

Most shopping centres are likely to be on multiple levels so you will encounter stairs, escalators and lifts. It would be prudent to try to get ahead of the target by having a team member waiting on the next floor up.

When dealing with multiple levels clarity of communications is even more important. Standard practice would be to refer to the ground floor as just that – 'ground floor', with the next level up being 'white 1', 'white 2' and so on. Any floors below ground floor are referred to as 'black 1', 'black 2' and so on. However you decide to do it, the most important thing is that it is clear and understood by all involved to avoid confusion. Let's consider this in practical terms. If the target enters a shopping centre on the ground floor and remains there, an operator should be deployed to 'white 1'. This affords not only a good overall awareness of the target and the wider environment but also means the team are prepared and well placed if the target gets on an escalator and goes up to 'white 1'. Remember, at all times it is important to remain outside the '10 to 2' arc.

Given the unique challenges posed by escalators and lifts, it is worth considering in a little more detail some things to remember in these scenarios.

Lifts

Consider the risks of sending a team member into such a confined environment with the target. There will be implications for them being seen and noticed. A dynamic risk assessment required, what is the likelihood of the target actually confronting the operative?

Remove any covert earpieces and ensure your phone is on silent. Avoid eye contact at all times.

Take control of the button panel. If it fits with the situation, you could consider asking which floor they want. Relay which floor you alight on to other team members as soon as safely practicable.

Escalators

Avoid putting more than one member of the team on an escalator at any one time. Once you are on you are locked in and lose flexibility to deploy if circumstances change. Where the escalator is crowded make use of the cover provided by other users.

Spacing is important. You do not want to be so close that you are compromising your cover but equally you cannot be so far back that the target has moved on and 'eyeball' lost as you remain on the escalator.

If the target reaches the top and promptly turns around and comes back down the adjacent escalator do not follow. You will immediately draw attention to yourself. Hand over to another team member and redeploy.

Parks and Open Spaces

These can present real challenges. By their very nature they are open with reduced opportunities for concealment. Try to keep your distance as far as practicable. Where possible, consider using a parallel pathway to the one used by the target rather than just walking behind them. Make a mental note of the location of benches, particularly useful if the target stops. In the absence of a bench and if the weather allows you may be able to just lay out on the grass. Consider what other people are doing, you don't want to be noticed.

Two Person Team (A, B Method)

In the commercial world, it is more likely that you would be operating as one half of a two person team. As the name above suggest, the basic principles remain exactly the same as for a three person team only operating as an A, B pairing rather than A, B and C. With reduced flexibility to interchange between operatives, it is even more important to remain flexible and alert to unexpected developments. Likewise, effective communication between you both is vital to ensure that you are making the best use of the resources available to you whilst minimising the risk of detection.

Summary of Foot Surveillance Tactics

Tell the team you are in control with, "I have…".

Always ask yourself if you are in the optimum position. If you aren't, move! Avoid eye contact with the target.

If the target approaches you, act naturally. Be prepared with a good cover story in the event you are questioned.

Always remember that being seen is not the same as being noticed.

If the target turns around, do not duck into doorways or behind hedges as this will only draw attention to yourself. Walk on, avoid eye contact and then reset.

Whenever you are in a confined space give yourself a reason for being there, make sure you are doing 'something'.

Do not take unnecessary risks. Sometimes it is better to take a loss to retain overall gain.

Stay out of the '10 to 2' arc, you will be noticed otherwise.

Keep good spatial awareness, particularly for other third parties who may be associated with the target but unknown to you.

Keep your phone on silent and Bluetooth deactivated.

Refresher Check

What are the three phases of a foot surveillance?

The 'arc of surveillance' is also known as the '10 to 4' arc. Is this true or false?

If the target enters a shopping centre on the ground floor and uses an escalator to go up two more floors, for the purposes of communicating his location to the rest of the team the target will be on:

A)   White 1.
B)   White 2.
C)   Black 2.

For safety reasons, Bluetooth on your phone should never be deactivated during an active follow. Is this true or false?

There are five scenarios listed when a 'change of eyeball' (handover) may be considered necessary. Can you list three of them?

If a target goes into a building the point of entry is always at:

A)   6 o'clock.
B)   12 o'clock.
C)   Whichever the operative feels most appropriate in the circumstances.

Any floors below the ground floor are always referred to using which colour?

A)   Black.
B)   White.
C)   Yellow.

Recommended Further Reading

'*The Theory of Covert Surveillance, The Surveillance Training Course Handbook*', Peter Jenkins (2020)

'*Covert Investigation*' (Sixth Edition, Blackstone's Practical Policing), Harfield and Harfield (2023)

'*Surveillance Tradecraft: The Professional's Guide to Covert Surveillance Training*', Peter Jenkins (2010)

'*Covert Surveillance: The Manual of Surveillance Training*', Peter Jenkins (1999)

Chapter Fourteen
Mobile Surveillance

Introduction

The professional private investigator will often rely on vehicle-based surveillance to gather evidence discreetly and lawfully. Whether tracking a subject in a bustling city or a quiet rural area, vehicles provide mobility, cover and flexibility. With the advance of modern technology there are a range of surveillance tactics which promise a more cost-effective return on investment in terms of time, effort and staffing levels, as well as safety and risk of compromise – most obviously OSINT and drones. However, there are times when a tried and tested tactic is the most appropriate for the circumstances and it is important to add this to the 'toolkit' of tactical options available for consideration. Mobile surveillance, therefore, remains a common tactic where an investigator follows a subject's vehicle while maintaining a low profile. Success hinges on the investigator's ability to remain undetected. Key strategies include the following:

- **Maintaining distance.** Staying several cars behind the target, using traffic lights, roundabouts and natural traffic flow to avoid suspicion.
- **Vehicle rotation.** Switching between multiple vehicles (for example, cars, motorcycles or bicycles) to prevent the target from recognising a single vehicle.
- **Teamwork.** Deploying two investigators in separate vehicles to alternate leads, reducing the risk of detection.

In practical terms, for example, in highly congested urban areas like any of the inner cities in the UK, an investigator might use a motorcycle to navigate busy streets, while a partner in a car follows at a distance using real-time GPS updates.

However, investigators must navigate strict legal frameworks, including the Data Protection Act 2018, General Data Protection Regulation and the Regulation of Investigatory Powers Act 2000, to ensure their methods comply with privacy laws. In this chapter we will consider some of the principal vehicle surveillance tactics employed by investigators, alongside practical considerations and, importantly, legal and ethical boundaries. As with the other chapters on surveillance, only a basic introduction to the subject can be covered here and students are encouraged to familiarise themselves with the recommended reading at the end of this chapter.

> **Learning Outcomes**
>
> By the end of this section you will:
>
> - Have a good understanding of the pros and cons of mobile surveillance as a tactical option.
>
> - Have learnt about the desired characteristics of a good surveillance vehicle.
>
> - Understand the importance of an effective and professional commentary with some tips for what to say and when to say it.
>
> - Have learnt about handovers – when is a good opportunity to handover and when a handover should be avoided.
>
> - Have learnt more about what to do when the target vehicle stops.
>
> - Have improved your awareness of some of the counter-surveillance techniques a person being followed may employ as well as different considerations for urban and rural settings.
>
> - Have learnt about how to respond to an eventual loss of contact.
>
> - Be aware of the important legal and ethical considerations of mobile surveillance.

Surveillance Teams

Any form of 'real world' surveillance is a team effort, not only in terms of practical considerations to reduce the risk of detection but also because of safety. In a vehicle-based mobile surveillance scenario this is especially important given the obvious challenges of following a vehicle in traffic whilst maintaining safety, avoiding detection and, importantly, observing the laws of the road. The simple rule of thumb with mobile surveillance is that the more operatives involved the greater the chances of a successful outcome. Equally, reliance should not be placed upon one mode of transport only. A combination of cars, vans and or motorcycles provides a much greater degree of flexibility to respond to a changing operational environment. Obviously there are important resource implications to be considered for any professional investigator recommending this tactic to a client, but safety and legal compliance should never be compromised. The absolute bare minimum resource for this tactic would be two operatives in two vehicles.

The other important thing to remember from this is that a mobile surveillance is precisely the opposite of that shown on TV and in the movies. Staff engaged in this tactic should be driving in a completely unobtrusive manner – no handbrake turns, no screeching of brakes or revving of engines. The manner of driving should not attract attention of either the subject of the surveillance nor the authorities, including the omni-present speed cameras and CCTV. The professional investigator needs to be able to anticipate what is happening in the traffic flow ahead. For example, is a traffic light likely to change after the target vehicle has gone past but before the operative can follow? Also, it is not practicable to drive in such a thoughtful manner and communicate effectively with the second vehicle. These are just some of the factors which make mobile surveillance more than simply 'following' somebody as they drive around. It takes practise and restraint.

In practical terms, before a mobile surveillance is adopted other tactical options should always be considered on grounds of both safety, effectiveness and cost. A more realistic option might be OSINT, a tracking device or indeed a static OP between two points. These options should always be considered and actively ruled out before resorting to a mobile surveillance.

Surveillance Vehicles

Surveillance vehicles should be ordinary and unremarkable. They should also be different to one another. The ideal surveillance vehicle is a common make and model, a dark colour that is commonly used, a minimum of a 1600cc engine, is safe and roadworthy and, importantly, is comfortable for the operatives using it in the event of a long shift. For example, does it have air conditioning? An effective heating system?

To avoid recognition, investigators often modify vehicles or adopt roles:

- **Rental vehicles.** Frequently rotating hire cars to prevent subjects from memorising license plates.
- **Taxis or ride-sharing.** Blending into ride-hailing services in cities, where passengers and drivers are less likely to be scrutinised.
- **Utility vans.** Using vehicles resembling those of telecom or energy companies, which are common in neighbourhoods and less likely to raise suspicion.

Adding props like traffic cones, high-vis jackets or clipboards reinforces the 'worker' disguise during static surveillance.

Mobile Commentary

Another practical reason for having more than one operative in each vehicle is to enable effective comms between vehicles. The driver will have their hands full driving and anticipating what is likely to happen on the road ahead without having to think about comms as well. Also a second person in the vehicle provides flexibility if a rapid foot deployment is required.

Providing a mobile commentary is important to ensure that the vehicles engaged in the operation are working together as part of a team, and handovers are smooth and unobtrusive. Commentary should be precise, factual and immediate. Repetition should be avoided unless it is conveying important information, such as a change of direction ('left, left, left') or another significant event has occurred and the lead vehicle is making a dynamic assessment ('standby, standby'). Remember the operatives who are the intended recipients of the commentary may not be able to actually see what is being described so brevity and accuracy are important. In summary, elements of a commentary that should always be conveyed to the rest of the team include:

- Direction of travel.
- Speed.
- Intentions to turn (as suggested by the use of indicators).
- Deviations (for example, last minute changes of direction).
- Anything unusual (particularly if this suggests a possible discovery).
- Loss of contact (even if only temporary).

It is worth looking at some of these elements of an effective commentary in more detail. The direction of travel should always be referenced against large landmarks, for example, a church or statue that can be easily seen when travelling at speed. Street names or other smaller signs cannot be easily seen and may be temporarily obscured by other road users. Likewise, the terms 'left' or 'right' should only be used to indicate change of direction and not to reference a landmark – operatives in a following vehicle may not be sharing the same visual cues as the lead vehicle if they are too far behind.

Use of indicators are precisely that, an indication of a change of direction. The more notice you can give of this impending change the better as it allows for any appropriate lane changes. Likewise it is good practice to give colleagues following behind warning of potential obstacles. These could include traffic lights, roundabouts, slow moving vehicles or anything else which may cause a challenge or delay. A good practical example of this might be where the lead vehicle sees a pedestrian approaching a crossing controlled by lights. They haven't pressed the lights yet but it is clear their intention is to do so once they reach the crossing. It may be appropriate for the following vehicle to speed up (provided it is safe to do so) to allow them a better chance to get through the lights before they change to allow the pedestrian right of way to cross the road.

Speed is always an important factor. It is fundamental to the overall safety of the operation not only for those in any of the vehicles involved but also pedestrians, cyclists and all other road users. In police pursuits, the speed of the vehicle being followed is always a critical element in dynamically risk assessing whether to continue or to abort and it should be no different for professional private investigators. Speed limits should be strictly adhered to even if the target vehicle chooses to ignore them. A mobile surveillance is not a pursuit.

Handovers

Handovers are an important and very necessary element of any mobile surveillance. They should be smooth and unobtrusive. The decision to handover is made by the lead vehicle and should be considered under the following circumstances:

- As soon as possible from the outset of the surveillance. This not only reduces the likelihood of the target becoming aware of the initial vehicle behind him but also allows the other team members to get 'up to speed' with the operation.

- Whenever there are multiple changes of direction in short succession. This will highlight the fact that the target is being followed as it is unlikely in most circumstances that two random vehicles would be making the exact same changes in direction of travel.

- If the target vehicle pulls over to the side of the road, lay-by, car park or similar. The lead vehicle should keep going and handover.

- For any other reason of compromise. A compromise need not necessarily terminate the operation but, for obvious reasons, does severely limit its effectiveness. This is an operational decision based upon all of the circumstances at the time.

Any environment will naturally present some obvious locations where a handover can be conducted smoothly including near-side junctions, petrol stations, roundabouts and lay-bys. Whichever of these is used, the lead vehicle should usually then take up position as the following vehicle after their colleagues have taken over as lead. It is always important, however, to only do so once you are no longer in the mirrors of the target vehicle.

When Not to Handover

Operational necessity may require a handover to occur when it is less than desirable so there can be no hard and fast rules here. However, there are some situations which should always be avoided as far as practicable:

- When turning into offside junctions.
- Whilst at traffic lights.
- Where traffic is heavy and manoeuvrability may be challenging.
- Whenever the traffic conditions are so light that any activity between vehicles may be obviously observed in a rear view mirror.

Responding to Stops

Whenever the target vehicle makes a substantive stop (as opposed to a temporary stop, for example, at traffic lights) this information must be relayed to the following vehicle as they may need to take over if the lead vehicle has to continue on. A stop under these circumstances moves the operation from a mobile surveillance to the so-called 'housing' phase. This can then become either a foot surveillance or a plotting up and resetting of vehicles ready to resume a mobile surveillance. This is an operational decision for the team leader based on the circumstances at the time and the requirements of the investigation. In re-setting, however, it is an obvious opportunity to change lead vehicles, get settled whilst remaining alert and generally ensure that you are ready to continue as a team in the optimum configuration possible. In this situation, a good team leader will be using this time to run through various 'what if' scenarios with the rest of the team.

The street plans below show a basic response to a stop where the target red vehicle is being surveilled by the grey flat truck with a back-up vehicle shown as a white van. In this straightforward scenario the lead vehicle continues past the target whilst the back-up vehicle pulls over and either plots up waiting for the subject to return or else one of the occupants commences a follow on foot, as shown on overleaf.

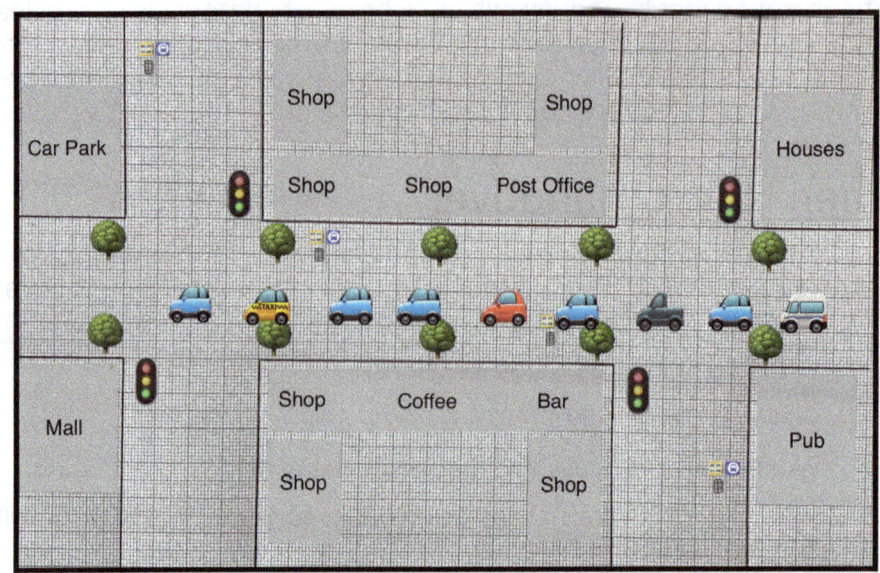

Lead and back-up vehicles following red target vehicle.

Counter-Surveillance Detection

Experienced subjects may check for tails, requiring investigators to anticipate and counteract their manoeuvres:

Target vehicle pulls over, lead vehicle overshoots, back-up vehicle takes over.

- Awareness of 'heat' zones: recognising when a target is driving erratically (for example, sudden U-turns, circling blocks) to spot surveillance.
- Using public transport: temporarily abandoning the vehicle to follow on foot or by train, then reuniting with a partner in a different car.
- False destinations: parking near landmarks or shopping centres to create plausible reasons for being stationary.

Rural Versus Urban Tactics

Tailoring methods to the environment is critical. In urban areas heavy traffic and pedestrians provide natural cover, but congestion and ANPR cameras pose challenges. Motorcycles or bicycles may be preferable for narrow streets. In rural areas, however, the considerations are different.

Fewer vehicles increase the risk of detection, so investigators might use farm vehicles or park in lay-bys under the guise of hiking or photography.

Loss of Contact

One of the 'what ifs' that always has to be considered is the loss of contact, particularly where during a mobile surveillance the decision has been made to plot up and await the target's return to their vehicle. Equally, given the inherent risks associated with mobile surveillance, the loss of contact scenario is always a distinct possibility and another reason why mobile surveillance may not be the most appropriate tactical option. A vehicle tracker may be a good contingency in the event of a loss as it will allow for a speedy resumption of an operation.

In the event of a loss, the least worst option is to continue along what would have been the most logical route. In a two vehicle operation each vehicle should split along nearside and offside to turnings to maximise the chances of picking up the target again. Common sense must prevail as to how long these different routes are followed and this will vary on the circumstances of the operation. As a last resort, members of the team could be re-tasked to places the target is known to frequent, for example, a place of work or home address.

In the event of a total loss, the decision will have to be made to stand down. Good practice would be to rendezvous with the team at a safe place that is a sufficient distance away from where the target vehicle may reasonably be supposed to be and to conduct a 'hot debrief'.

Legal and Ethical Boundaries

As with any form of surveillance it is of paramount importance that the professional investigator is compliant with UK privacy and surveillance laws. Principally these will include the following:

- Regulation of Investigatory Powers Act 2000, whereby investigators must ensure surveillance is proportionate and necessary, avoiding intrusion into private spaces such as homes or gardens.
- General Data Protection Act 2018, which mandates that all personal data collected during surveillance (for example, photos, videos, location data) must be processed lawfully, stored securely and deleted when no longer necessary.
- Human Rights Act 1998 (Article 8), which protects an individual's right to privacy. Surveillance must not unjustifiably infringe on this right.

Complying with the law naturally places restrictions upon the methods available to the investigator. For example, trespassing without consent is illegal so surveillance must take place from public spaces. GPS tracking requires explicit consent from the vehicle owner and installing trackers without permission violates data protection laws. Likewise recording conversations without consent from all parties is prohibited under the Investigatory Powers Act 2016 and RIPA. Accessing phones, emails or social media accounts without authorisation breaches the Computer Misuse Act 1990. Other prohibited actions include persistent or intimidating surveillance, which may constitute an offence under the Protection from Harassment Act 1997. Impersonation of a law enforcement official is also an offence.

Best practice for ethical mobile surveillance could be summarised thus:

- **Public spaces.** Conduct surveillance from streets, parks or other areas with no expectation of privacy.
- **Use of technology.** Dash-cams or body-cams are permissible in public but avoid capturing private property.
- **Consent for tracking.** Secure written consent from the vehicle owner before using GPS trackers.
- **Regular training:** Stay updated on evolving laws and technology.

By balancing legal compliance with ethical integrity, UK private investigators can effectively conduct mobile surveillance while respecting individual rights and maintaining professional credibility.

Challenges and Solutions

- **Automatic Number Plate Recognition (ANPR) cameras.** ANPR systems can log an investigator's vehicle, alerting 'surveillance-savvy' subjects. Using unmarked or rental cars mitigates this.
- **Time constraints.** Long shifts require planning for fuel, rest breaks and shift rotations to maintain alertness.
- **Weather.** In adverse conditions, subjects may stay indoors. Infrared tech or waterproof gear helps to maintain surveillance.

Conclusion

Vehicle surveillance remains a cornerstone of private investigation in the UK, combining traditional shadowing techniques with modern technology. Success depends on meticulous planning, adaptability and strict adherence to the law. By blending into their surroundings, leveraging teamwork and respecting privacy boundaries, investigators can gather compelling evidence while avoiding legal pitfalls. Ultimately, the balance between persistence and discretion defines the art of effective surveillance.

Vehicle Surveillance Training Exercise: The 'Lost Cat' Scenario

This exercise focuses on the practical application of vehicle surveillance techniques while adhering to UK legal and ethical considerations.

Scenario

A local resident, Mrs Higgins, reports her beloved cat, Mr Whiskers, missing. She suspects her neighbour, Mr Grumbles, who has openly expressed a dislike for cats, may have taken him. Mrs Higgins has hired your agency to discreetly investigate. Your task is to conduct vehicle surveillance on Mr Grumbles to ascertain if he's involved in Mr Whiskers's disappearance.

Objectives

- Conduct covert vehicle surveillance while maintaining legal and ethical boundaries.
- Identify and record relevant vehicle details.
- Practise following a vehicle discreetly and safely.
- Document observations accurately and concisely.
- Understand the limitations of vehicle surveillance and the importance of corroborating evidence.

Equipment

- Notepads and pens/pencils (for manual note-taking).
- Mobile phones with recording capabilities (audio and video). Inform students of data protection and privacy implications of recording.
- Maps of the local area.
- Binoculars (optional).

Exercise Setup

Briefing. Explain relevant UK laws regarding privacy, data protection and public space surveillance. Emphasise the importance of avoiding trespass, harassment and any illegal activity. Discuss considerations regarding privacy.

Vehicle identification. Provide students with a description of Mr Grumbles's vehicle (make, model, colour, registration if available). Discuss methods for identifying the correct vehicle discreetly.

Surveillance point selection. Guide students in selecting appropriate observation points near Mr Grumbles's residence. Consider factors like visibility, distance and potential for being observed.

Stress the importance of public access and avoiding private property.

Surveillance Execution

Students take turns conducting surveillance for a set period, for example, one hour. They should record the time they begin surveillance as well as noting any activity around Mr Grumbles's residence. If the vehicle leaves, attempt to follow discreetly, maintaining a safe distance and adhering to traffic laws. Emphasise that losing the subject vehicle is acceptable as safety is paramount. Discuss 'leap-frogging' techniques if appropriate. Record the vehicle's route (major roads/landmarks), destination (if possible) and any occupants. Note the time surveillance ends.

Debriefing

After the surveillance period, bring the students together to discuss their experiences. Focus on the following:

- What information did they gather?
- Were there any challenges encountered?
- Did they observe anything suspicious?
- Did they maintain legal and ethical boundaries?
- How could they improve their techniques?
- What are the next steps in the investigation (for example, further surveillance, database checks, interviewing)?

Important Considerations

Realism versus legality. Make it clear that this is a training exercise. Students should not engage in any real surveillance outside of the exercise parameters.

Data protection. Emphasise the importance of handling any collected information responsibly and in accordance with data protection laws. Discuss secure storage and disposal of data.

Ethical considerations. Reinforce the ethical implications of surveillance and the importance of respecting individual privacy.

Safety. Prioritise the safety of the students at all times. Stress the importance of adhering to traffic laws and avoiding any risky behaviour.

Adaptability. This scenario can be adapted to different levels of experience and can incorporate additional elements, such as counter-surveillance awareness.

This exercise provides a practical introduction to vehicle surveillance for trainee private investigators in the UK, emphasising legal and ethical considerations alongside practical skills. It is crucial to remember that real-world investigations often involve more complex situations and require a thorough understanding of the law.

Refresher Check

Can you list three of the key pieces of legislation professional investigators in the UK must take into consideration when engaging in any form of covert surveillance?

When considering mobile surveillance, what are some of the other tactical options an investigator should consider which may be more effective, cheaper and safer whilst still achieving the objectives of the investigation?

In considering a vehicle for use during a mobile surveillance, what are some of the characteristics an investigator should always consider?

What are the various elements of a commentary that should always be conveyed to the rest of the team?

The decision to handover is made by the lead vehicle and should be considered under what circumstances?

There were four scenarios listed where a handover should not be considered. Can you name three of them?

How might a target employ counter-surveillance measures?

Recommended Further Reading

'*The Theory of Covert Surveillance, The Surveillance Training Course Handbook*', Peter Jenkins (2020)

'*Covert Investigation*', (Sixth Edition, Blackstone's Practical Policing) Harfield and Harfield (2023)

'*Surveillance Tradecraft: The Professional's Guide to Covert Surveillance Training*', Peter Jenkins (2010)

'*Covert Surveillance: The Manual of Surveillance Training*', Peter Jenkins (1999)

Chapter Fifteen
And Finally...

Introduction

So... if you've made it this far then perhaps you really do want to become a private investigator. In this book we have endeavoured to provide a relatively brief overview of the key skills and considerations before entering the business, whether you have similar skill sets from a previous career or you are completely new to the profession. In what is still a relatively unregulated business, we have tried to emphasise the notion of the *professional* private investigator, adhering not only to existing UK law but also certain principles of good practice. In this chapter we will look at some of the personal qualities required but also consider methodology – how you approach your business by applying a solid step-by-step approach.

The Method

Effective information gathering is crucial to the success of the investigation and it starts from the moment you are notified of a new case or are planning on meeting with a prospective client. Understanding the client's needs is essential and will involve asking questions, listening and collecting data (gathering information). Taking a systematic approach to information gathering will allow you to collect, organise and analyse the data resulting in you being able to make informed decisions and start a comprehensive investigation.

The '5W+H' questions are a solid approach to assisting you in gathering information and gaining a broad understanding of the case or client's needs from the very outset to better inform your investigation plan:

- **What:** asks for a thing or idea.
- **Why:** asks for a reason.
- **Where:** asks for a location.
- **When:** asks for a date or time.
- **Who:** asks for target details.
- **How:** asks for a method or process.

One of the first steps to understanding your client's needs and expectations is to *ask* the right questions. You need to understand their goals, concerns, budget, timeline and scope of work. You also need to clarify any assumptions, expectations or constraints that might affect your investigation to better achieve their desired outcomes. Be very clear from the outset to ensure you understand your client's desired outcomes.

Meeting the Client

Before meeting with your client, you should be aware that most people have distinct needs:

- Visual.
- Emotional.
- Functional.
- Financial.

Visual

People will have preferences for the visual input that surrounds them and it is well documented that people can make decisions in a matter of minutes based on what they see. It is therefore essential that you consider this when arranging to meet the client at a location and you should also be conscious of what impact the way you are dressed will have on the client.

Emotional

You must understand that by taking the decision to employ a private investigator most people are likely to be in a heightened state of emotion and may be upset, angry, jealous, frustrated and so on. This should be factored in when managing the expectations of the client.

Functional

This is really important when addressing the expectations of the client as what you say you can do actually has to work and deliver an outcome that progresses the investigation. Remember not to make any promises to the client that you will not be able to deliver on.

Financial

From the client's standpoint, the cost of your product or service has to be within their ability to pay. This is why it is important for you to understand the financial position of the client. Preparing quality reports, maintaining regular contact and providing quick results will help you to create a solid reputation within the private investigation world.

Report Preparation

The 'STAR process' when applied to reports means structuring your written account of an event or accomplishment by outlining the following:
- Situation.
- Task.
- Action.
- Result.

This will provide context, enabling you to describe the goal, detail the steps you took and highlighting the positive outcomes achieved. This method is often used to effectively communicate achievements and demonstrate competency in reports, particularly when detailing specific examples or experiences.

Breakdown of the 'STAR process' in reports:

- **Situation.** Briefly explain the context of the information that you know and include background information provided by the client.
- **Task.** Clearly state the specific goal or objective you were tasked with accomplishing within the situation.
- **Action.** Describe the specific actions you took to address the task, highlighting your key contributions and decision-making process.
- **Result.** Conclude by outlining the positive outcomes achieved as a result of your actions, including measurable data or feedback where applicable. Why use STAR in a report? The format provides clarity and conciseness. The structured format helps you to present information in a clear and organised manner, making it easy for the reader to understand your contributions. Impactful storytelling is another facet of this format. By focusing on specific examples, you can effectively showcase your skills and achievements in a compelling narrative. Lastly, credibility and objectivity. Providing concrete details about your actions and results adds credibility to your report.

Log of Enquiries

Logging all enquiries, regardless of the quality or potential of those enquiries, is vitally important as it forms the basis of all information gathered and allows you to maintain accurate records of what you were told and what you did. So, what do you need to record about each enquiry you receive? We advise recording as much of the following information as possible:

- Date of enquiry.
- Time of enquiry (as close as possible).
- Contact method (for example, phone, email, enquiry form).
- Basic details about the enquirer (name, phone and so on).
- What the enquiry was about (for example, cheating husband).
- What action you took.
- Outcomes.

How do you record your enquiry log? There are several ways but ideally use whatever works best for you, as long as it is easily retrievable. Some recommended methods would include:

- **Spreadsheet.** If only a couple of people are responsible for logging enquiries then a spreadsheet could be the answer.
- **Shared document.** If it's likely that more people will log enquiries, then an online shared document would work because that allows multiple people to use the same document. Most people would use the free Google Sheets.

Remember to ensure that your enquiry log is up-to-date, accurate and legible, and be careful what you record as it could be disclosable in future criminal prosecutions.

Personal Qualities

However, over and above all of that there is a range of qualities you will need to maintain your own personal and professional resilience. In this chapter we will look at some of those as well as providing some examples of why we think this is such a rewarding business to be in, namely those cases where if you told somebody what you had done at work that day, they simply wouldn't believe you!

Being an effective, professional private investigator in the UK requires a distinctive set of personal qualities and characteristics that enable individuals to tackle intricate cases, maintain professionalism and satisfy client expectations. This demanding profession, shaped by legal frameworks, such as the UK General Data Protection Regulation and the Police and Criminal Evidence Act 1984 (PACE), calls for a blend of intellectual, ethical and interpersonal strengths.

Foremost among these is analytical thinking. Private investigators must possess a keen ability to dissect complex information (be it surveillance footage, financial records, or witness statements) to uncover the truth.

For instance, when investigating a corporate fraud case, the professional investigator might meticulously cross-reference expense reports with travel logs to detect discrepancies. This sharp, detail-oriented mindset, ensures that evidence is robust and defensible, whether presented to a client or in a legal context. The professional investigator must always keep in mind whether the information being collected is ever likely to be required as evidence. If so, it must be admissible. To be admissible it must have been obtained lawfully.

Equally essential are discretion and integrity. The sensitive nature of the work, ranging from matrimonial disputes to workplace misconduct, demands absolute confidentiality and adherence to ethical and legal boundaries. A single misstep, such as unauthorised data collection, could violate UK GDPR, invalidate findings and expose the investigator to penalties. Effective investigators build trust by consistently demonstrating professionalism and respecting privacy, a principle reinforced through training that stresses compliance with legislation like PACE. For example, when conducting surveillance, they must balance investigative needs with the subject's rights, ensuring their methods are lawful and proportionate. We have endeavoured to make clear that professional investigators will comply with legislation even where there may be no clear requirement for them to do so.

Strong communication skills are another cornerstone. Investigators interact with a wide range of people, from distressed clients seeking answers to reluctant witnesses requiring gentle persuasion. The ability to conduct a structured interview or draft a precise, evidence-based report is critical. During a professional discussion, an investigator might need to explain ethical dilemmas clearly to demonstrate sound judgment. Adaptability in tone and approach, whether calming an anxious client or negotiating access to information, distinguishes an effective investigator.

Finally, resilience and patience are indispensable. Investigations often involve long hours, unpredictable outcomes and dead ends. An investigator tracking a missing person might spend weeks piecing together fragmented clues, facing setbacks like uncooperative contacts or elusive leads. This tenacity, coupled with the patience to wait for the right moment (such as observing a subject's routine during surveillance) ensures thoroughness. Investigators must be able to stay focused under pressure.

Additionally, curiosity and initiative drive success. Effective investigators proactively seek answers, exploring unconventional angles (like tracing a subject's social media footprint) while staying within legal limits. This inquisitiveness fuels creative problem-solving, a trait vital for unravelling complex cases.

In conclusion, an effective, professional private investigator blends analytical prowess, unwavering integrity, adept communication, resilience, patience and curiosity. These qualities, cultivated through rigorous training, equips the professional investigator to excel in a profession that demands both skill and character, delivering justice and clarity in equal measure.

And Finally…

There's no substitute for hearing direct testimony straight from the horse's mouth so to speak because it's impossible to legislate for every eventuality. Being a private investigator will inevitably surprise you, test you and make you question everything you thought was the right approach, no matter what it tells you in any book. So here it is. Straight from the mouth of the horse…

The Curious Case of the Diamond Earrings

We had an enquiry from a wealthy couple who had lost or misplaced a pair of diamond earrings worth a whopping £65k. Unfortunately, they were uninsured. The couple was certain that the last place they had seen the earrings was somewhere in their family home. Most likely, they thought, in their bedroom. They reached out to us, hoping we could help them not only with the search but also as they had a suspicion they may have been taken… I reassured them we had experience of conducting all manner of searches in a wide range of environments during many of our previous investigations. Of course, that wasn't entirely true as the circumstances surrounding this case were quite unique. This is where having a standard set of procedures no matter the nature of the enquiry comes in handy. After following the usual procedures we were able to form a workable plan for our investigation. As previously mentioned, whilst they suspected or thought they had misplaced them, they couldn't rule out the possibility their full-time housekeeper may have stolen them.

The wife was sure she had left the earrings out on a side dresser before they went away for a couple of days. However, when they came back, they were not there, and the housekeeper claimed she hadn't seen them there either. Whilst the wife was sure she hadn't left them out, she couldn't be 100% sure, especially since they had a long and good previous relationship with the housekeeper. The wife and the housekeeper would often sit together and chat, or while the housekeeper was working, so had become almost a friend to the wife, this meant before they could confront or accuse the housekeeper they had to be sure.

Our brief was to search the house in the hope of finding the missing diamond earrings, failing that to investigate the staff, specifically the housekeeper. I borrowed some handheld metal detector wands and along with the rest of the team made a plan to search the house. In the event the search didn't reveal the diamond earrings, the plan was to pivot and focus on investigating the housekeeper. I had asked the clients to make sure the housekeeper thought the diamond earrings were insured, and would be present when we were due to call and conduct the search, also that we were there in the capacity of acting on behalf of their insurance company. Of course, there was no insurance so this was all a ruse to fool the housekeeper.

We did a thorough house search using both good old eyeball and the handheld metal detectors systematically going from room to room. This helped us determine if the diamond earrings were simply misplaced or something more suspicious. As we weren't able to find them during the search phase our attention then turned towards the housekeeper and other staff members. At this point I would like to just briefly mention client management: Since we were going to be conducting a full house search, I suggested to the clients that they might want to go through the house themselves beforehand and remove any items they didn't want us to see (sensitive documents, adult toys in the bedroom, etc.). Considerations towards your clients helps engender trust and is clearly in your clients' best interests, i.e. in this instance helping them to avoid any embarrassment and should always be considered especially if they hadn't previously thought about it...

Prior to arriving at the house, I had printed out a large, technical looking document that was in reality cut and pasted from my home BT phone account terms and conditions section of the website. I then added a front sheet with the logo and name of the (well known) 'insurance company' and separate section at the back of this very formal legal looking document for the couple to sign. Ostensibly this was designed to give the impression of a waiver and legally entitling us to search the house and to carry out any investigations we thought were necessary as part of the claims process and as mentioned, were all designed to be part of the show that further convinced the housekeeper we were there acting for the insurance company.

Of course, this was just another bluff and part of the bigger plan. I had also briefed the actual clients I was going to be quite strict with them citing warnings such as insurance fraud and that once they had signed, we had the right to do whatever we thought was best in retrieving the items and/or settling the claim.

Once they had signed the waiver the plan was for my team to get on with the search and the couple to also leave the room for whatever reason. This just left myself and the housekeeper in the room.

I wanted to have five minutes alone with the housekeeper in order to have a relaxed conversation and plant the seed that we were there to investigate a possible insurance fraud and/or uncover information that could lead to the recovery of the diamond earrings. My clients (the 'insurance company') were not very keen to pay out £65k. And as such would be prepared to pay out a substantial reward for information that would lead to either the retrieval of the diamond earrings or evidence that could prove a fraud had taken place. And furthermore, this could all be done confidentially on a no further questions asked basis. Basically, I wanted her to know I didn't care where the information came from, they just didn't want to pay out £65k.

After planting this seed, I joined the rest of my team and we genuinely carried out a really thorough search of the house – we needed to set a baseline to make sure they weren't, after all, just misplaced.

A couple of days later, I received a call from the housekeeper asking if I could pay a visit to her at her home address of which, of course, I agreed.

When I arrived at the housekeeper's home address she invited me in, everything was very friendly and chatty. She handed me a hand written document in the form of a log, dates, times, duration etc to read through whilst she was making me a cup of tea. Scanning through the document it immediately became obvious that it was in fact quite a detailed log covering the wife's (mainly daytime) drinking habits and the frequency of the couple's arguments and general substance of what they argued about. The log covered a period of months, not weeks, and was clear that some effort had been put into it running, as it did, to some 20+ pages.

During my chat with the housekeeper I explained that the insurance company wasn't interested in how much they drank or what they argued about, all they were concerned about was collecting evidence of fraud or information that would lead to the recovery of the diamond earrings and ultimately avoid paying out the £65k value. I offered to make a confidential payment to help achieve either of these goals and I left the house making sure to take the dossier with me.

The following day I received another phone call from the housekeeper only this time to tell me she had 'remembered' seeing the diamond earrings mixed up with some other jewellery on top of the wife's dresser. Now having conducted the full search and set the baseline I knew that couldn't be true. Nonetheless, I informed the couple (AKA the real clients) of this information and sure enough after checking, there they were! (We had also installed a few covert cameras around the house, one of which covered the area of the dresser and the missing diamond earrings being found.)

Upon checking the footage it clearly showed the housekeeper dusting that area then removing something wrapped in tissue paper from her pocket and placing it among the other items on the dresser!). It is important to note at this stage that from the footage you could not see the diamonds, just the actions of the housekeeper and the removal of 'something' wrapped up in tissue paper. I'll come back to why that is relevant later...

So, case closed? Well yes but also not quite. It's an important part of your role, especially if you decide to start your own agency, to remember you are there to support your clients throughout the process not just in fulfilling the brief they have asked you to but to go beyond. Remember our clients usually come to us because they are facing problems they can't handle on their own, they rely on our guidance and experience.

In this case, it was clear the housekeeper couldn't stay with the couple as all semblance of trust had been destroyed. Because we didn't have the evidence that categorically proved the housekeeper had a) stolen the diamond earrings and b) then replaced them from her pocket back on to the dresser, we needed a legal means with which to sack her. And, yes you guessed it... This is where the dossier came in handy.

I contacted the housekeeper and requested she attend our offices on the pretence of collecting her reward for the recovery of the diamond earrings. In reality it was a neutral venue whereby the husband would be waiting and formally dismiss her from their employment using the breach of her NDA (non-disclosure agreement) as the justification making no reference to the diamond earrings and suspected theft at all.

As well as wanting to avoid any further disruption to the family home I thought the use of a neutral venue preferable as I additionally felt we also had a duty of care towards the housekeeper, so I didn't want her to feel completely hijacked and overly vulnerable. Afterwards, I made sure one of my female team members stayed with her until her husband came to pick her up. I couldn't change what she did, but I thought it was important to treat her with respect and as a human being with feelings and mindful there may be unknown personal circumstances that might have led her to act the way she did.

This job takes you to places where you'll explore the depths of human emotions. Even though you're representing your clients' best interests and following their instructions, you should always act respectfully and try to avoid causing any unnecessary harm. Why? Because it's the right thing to do.

Mike Jennings, Founder of Cotswold Private Investigations

www.ingramcontent.com/pod-product-compliance
Lightning Source LLC
Chambersburg PA
CBHW071711020426
42333CB00017B/2220